SET FREE TO BE

Manfred T. Brauch

JUDSON PRESS, VALLEY FORGE

LAKE
VIEW
BOOKS

Lake View Books are books of outstanding merit and broad interest which originated at the American Baptist Assembly, Green Lake, Wisconsin. The material on which this book is based was presented under the Boardman Lectureship at Green Lake.

SET FREE TO BE

Library of Congress Cataloging in Publication Data

Brauch, Manfred T.
  Set free to be.

  1. Bible. N.T. Romans—Criticism, interpretation, etc. I. Title.
BS2665.2.B73   227'.1'07   75-4721
ISBN 0-8170-0663-X

Printed in the U.S.A.

Contents

Dedication:
To the memory of my
father
who has passed from
the desert of decision
into the Promised Land.

Introduction

In one of the best-known passages of Scripture, 2 Corinthians 5:17, Paul affirms for his Christian audience a central conviction of the early church, namely, that by means of Jesus' presence in first-century Palestine something radically new had become possible for humankind:

> If any one is in Christ, he is a new creation; the old has passed away, behold, the new has come.

Indeed, the entire New Testament reverberates with the joyful proclamation that in the Christ event, God had broken into history. The world was no longer the same. A new age had dawned upon human existence. The "principalities" and "powers" which had dominated the "old age" had been defeated. Therefore Paul's liberating conclusion was, "For freedom Christ has set us free" (Galatians 5:1). The first Christians were liberated by that emancipation proclamation and energized by the affirmation that God had released into the world his creating and re-creating Spirit. As the Spirit of God had once moved over chaos and created order, so now he had created and was creating a new order in the midst of the chaos of human history.

But these first Christians also recognized that, in many ways, the "old" remained with them, and the "new" which dominated their horizon at the beginning of their Christian existence needed to be reaffirmed and appropriated again and again. These early Christians wrestled with the reality of Rome and the oppressive power of its domination. Injustice and immorality prevailed. They also had to come to terms with the realities of continuing bondage in personal Christian existence, with bitter strife within communal Christian existence, with the continuance of personal failure, of anxiety, of frustration, and of sin. "Why the old when the new is come?" So went the query as it emerged from the anguished struggle of early Christian experience. "Why are these things still with us? Why, if it is true that 'the old has passed away' and 'the new has come'?"

The cry of the saints under the altar in the Apocalypse (see Revelation 6:9-10)—"How long, O Lord?"—reflects the early Christians' mood of impatience with the reality that much of the world seemed to be going on as usual. And Paul's question, "How can we who died to sin still live in it?" reflects this frustration in the community. How is it possible to account for the presence of the "old" together with the "new"?

It must be said candidly that this problem is not confined to the first-generation Christians. The history of Christianity and Christian thinking (i.e., theology) shows the continuing struggle with and the constant tension between the affirmation of the new and the recognition of the continuing presence of the old. Christian faith—or more specifically, faith in Christ—ever stands in tension between the claim that in Christ a new humanity has been inaugurated and the painful awareness of that new humanity's continuing position under the shadow of the old humanity. The realization of the new humanity is always partial, and even the experience of the new life is constantly threatened by invasion from the realm of the old.

On the one hand we affirm life in Christ as a new kind of life-style, and then we are embarrassed to find so little difference between our actual life-style and that of our fellows who make no such affirmations. We claim the forgiveness of God for our imperfect existence and recognize how our living fails to radiate this reality. We worship the Christ who lived his life for others and discover we are often living our lives for ourselves. We proclaim allegiance to Christ as Lord while living by a list of priorities which indicates that there are indeed "many gods and lords" by which we *really* live.

How are we to understand this dilemma? How are we to deal with the reality of this tension which continually imposes itself upon Christian experience? Historically speaking, there have been two main ways in which Christians have sought to deal with the problem. Both ways have arisen out of the almost universal cliché that *the spirit is willing, but the flesh is weak.*

One response to this idea was a response which manifested itself as early as A.D. 50 in the Christian community at Corinth. It was the "spiritualizing" of Christian faith. The argument went something like this: "Since the body, the flesh, the corporeal aspect of humankind is at best weak, at worst corrupt, what we need to do is to concentrate on the spiritual side, on the soul. And since, through Christ, our souls have been redeemed, it really does not matter what we do with our bodies." It does not take much imagination to see where this kind of splitting of the human personality could lead. In Corinth, it led to libertinism, which manifested itself in a complete disregard for the moral-ethical life and a haughty disdain for the brother and sister who had not attained what was considered a liberated spirituality.

A second response to the affirmation that *the spirit is willing, but the flesh is weak* was one which manifested itself during Paul's missionary activity in Asia Minor. It was the "legalizing" of the Christian faith. The argument here went as follows: "The flesh really interferes with the attempt of the human spirit to be in perfect communion with God. Therefore, 'the flesh,' with all its passions and desires, must be made subservient to the spirit. We must impose—by means of codes of conduct—such close strictures upon our lives that the inner purity of the spirit is not somehow defiled by the flesh." The extreme form of this response was a rigorous asceticism and monastic isolation from entanglements with the world. The tragedy of Martin Luther, flagellating himself almost to the point of death in order to win God's favor, is a striking example of such an understanding of the meaning of Christian existence.

It would be easy for us simply to dismiss these responses as obvious misunderstandings of what the Christian faith is all about. But that would only be possible if we closed our eyes to the reality of our own situation, for an analysis of much that goes under the name "Christian" in our day reveals that the models of "libertinism" and "legalism" are still with us—though disguised in contemporary dress. We too often function under the shadow of the platitude: *the spirit is willing, but the flesh is weak.* Where it does not become an escape hatch from the demands of Christian discipleship, it forms the basis for either a disregard for bodily, concrete things and an elevation of the *spiritual* or a suppression of the physical with a view to the purification of the *soul.*

The contemporary version of the libertine model manifests itself in an often isolated preoccupation with confessional, affirmational, conceptual aspects of the Christian faith and, at the same time, a tendency to ignore the practical implication of those confessions and affirmations. It is large on correct doctrinal formulations, but fails to ask what these mean for concrete relationships in the world. It majors in lofty *spiritual experiences* and glorifies extraordinary *spiritual phenomena*, but minors in the attempt to bring these to bear on the crucial issues that face our families and our communities and our world. In effect, this way of dealing with the tension between what we affirm about our existence in the new humanity created in Christ and what we actually are decisively divorces Christian faith from life. The inevitable result is powerlessness and frustration.

The contemporary version of the legalistic model is an historical replica of the old, minus the monastic isolationism and with the addition of contemporary cultural baggage. Since our senses—the windows of our physical household—are corrupted by the Fall, a functional separation between *the world* and these senses must be brought about. Such a separation is facilitated by the imposition of an external code: "Do not touch; do not taste; do not handle!" The so-called "sins of the flesh" are naturally placed at the top of the list of prohibitions and often become the focus for moral judgment and condemnation by those who feel they have lived by the code. This religion by external conformity to a set of prohibitions results in a largely cold, joyless, loveless existence. Why? Because the internal compass which allows loving and dynamic response to one's neighbor is missing. We have all met persons in the Christian community who felt that they had all the correct Christian affirmations correctly wrapped up in a correct bundle, but who were not free to be lovingly present for their fellow human beings. That is a kind of tomb-existence which has nothing to do with what Paul calls "the glorious liberty of the children of God" (Romans 8:21).

If the above ways of dealing with the basic tension in Christian existence are erroneous, how then are we to understand the presence of that tension, how are we to account for it, and how are we to come to grips with it? By now it will have dawned upon the reader that this writer does not subscribe to the common cliché *the spirit is willing, but the flesh is weak.* To be sure, in the realm of mundane, everyday experience, the assertion reflects a universal recognition. It is true that physical exhaustion and a tired body are a hindrance to the accomplishments of higher goals which we have set for ourselves. But in the realm of religion, specifically in Christian existence, the above dictum is essentially un-Christian because it denies the comprehensiveness of God's redemptive purposes for human life.

There were Greek thinkers, prior to and contemporary with the birth of the Christian movement, who saw human physicalness—the body—as the prisonhouse or tomb of the soul, and who felt that salvation consisted of the liberation of a person's higher self, his or her spirit or soul, from its entrapment with the body. That mentality concerning human nature must be decidedly rejected on the basis of the biblical point of view, for in the witness of the New Testament we as *total persons* are the objects of God's redemptive purposes. In our totality as *physical-spiritual beings*, we are the objects of God's forgiving act in Christ. In our *wholeness*, we stand under the constraining love of Christ by which we can become new creations. In our *concrete existence*, we can be transformed into the image of Christ. The purpose of redemption, according to the New Testament, *is not* to fit the soul for its heavenly destination and to free it from its entanglements with the body, *but rather* to free us for life *within* the concrete physicalness in such a way that the Creator's purposes for human existence can be realized.

> In seeking to become angels
> we may become less than men.[1]

The *human person*—in the context of relationship to other human persons and to the totality of the created order—is the locus of God's intervention; to affirm less than that is to limit God, and the New Testament does not so limit him!

If, then, a splitting of the human personality into physicalness and spiritualness cannot legitimately be used as a causal factor for the tension created by the gap between Christian affirmation and Christian practice, what can? The biblical view of Christian existence *demands* the presence of that tension. That is to say, the salvation event *does not* produce a new personality, *but* a new situation. This new situation is Christian existence—an existence between the "already" and the "not-yet," between "being" and "becoming," between the *indicative* ("you are") and the *imperative* ("become what you are"), between "is-ness" and "ought-ness." The salvation event frees us to live life at the crossroads between obedience and disobedience, between the old humanity and the new humanity, between life and death, between religious captivity and religious freedom, between individual self-assertion and communal responsibility, between ego-directedness and other-directedness.

It is our purpose, in the chapters which follow, to take a look at the texts in Paul's letter to the Romans where these polarities emerge. We hope that a fresh understanding of these polarities in Christian existence will facilitate becoming *freed from* an often debilitating tension and *freed for* a creative tension.

CHAPTER 1

The New Possibility

The salvation event *does not* create a *new personality;* it creates a *new situation.* What is this salvation event? How shall we understand this new situation? The answers are to be found through taking a fresh look at Paul's understanding and use of the term, *the righteousness of God.* Discovering the Pauline perspective will hopefully help us come to grips with the new situation of the "justified" person.

Most serious readers of Paul's Letter to the Romans quickly discover that the passage in 1:16-17 contains, in miniature, the theme of the entire letter.

> . . . I am not ashamed of the gospel: it is the power of God for salvation to every one who has faith, to the Jew first and also to the Greek. For in it the righteousness of God is revealed through faith for faith. . . .

Among several key words and phrases in these two short verses—such as *gospel, power of God, salvation,* and *faith*—there is one term which in Romans dominates the scene, namely, *the righteousness of God.* Romans has aptly been called "the Gospel of the Righteousness of God." What meaning does Paul seek to convey by the use of this term?

In the interpretation of the biblical text, it simply will not do to begin with the assumption that words mean what they mean to us! For it is highly probable that our understanding of the meaning of a biblical term is not what the author intended in his or her use of it. One basic principle of biblical interpretation is that the meaning of a term may shift decidedly, depending on the way in which it is used as well as on the context in which it is located. Words and phrases have a history, and interpreters must take that history into consideration when they attempt to elicit the meaning of a text; for the words written *then* may have meant something different from what they mean *now*. That was precisely Martin Luther's problem with the phrase "the righteousness of God." He was virtually crushed because he understood the idea of God's righteousness "literally," until he realized that "righteousness" meant for Paul something entirely different than it meant in Latin or German and that it is much closer in meaning to what we call *grace*. Luther's potent insight has suffered the fate of grass which today is green and tomorrow is withered. It is the lost dynamic of Luther's insight which we must rediscover, for it is likely that the plain meaning of the word "righteousness"—which the English language has inherited by way of the Continent—does not convey the precise Pauline understanding.

Much of our thinking about God (i.e., theology) has been conditioned by centuries of Christian thought, born initially in the encounter of Christian affirmation with the Graeco-Roman world. That world was dominated by the Greek mind. Socrates and Plato and Aristotle had brought their legacy of rational inquiry, of the systematic analysis of reality. It was that legacy which ultimately prepared the soil for the explosion of scientific inquiry in the Occident. It was in this intellectual atmosphere that the early Christian thinkers creatively conveyed the meaning of their faith. The great church councils during the first centuries of the Christian era give evidence that our fathers in the faith attempted to communicate the essence of their faith in categories which corresponded to the Greek mind. Thus, where the New Testament witnesses were content to speak about the reality of the divine presence in terms of *God* or *Christ* or the *Spirit,* and often used these terms interchangeably without regard for precision, the deliberation of the church councils resulted in the formulation of the doctrine of the Trinity, in which the nature and the relationships and the functions of Father, Son, and Spirit were clearly defined and systematized. Again, where the biblical witnesses were largely content to speak about and to respond to the great acts of God, Christian thinkers, in confrontation with the Greek mind, proceeded to define and analyze God. Much of our thinking about God is traceable to that period in the history of the church. We need only to turn to a standard text on Christian doctrine or systematic theology and to open it to the section which deals with God. Here we are confronted immediately with a long list of attributes: God is all-powerful, all-knowing, all-present; he is transcendent, incomprehensible, unchanging; he is holy, just, loving, etc.

"Righteousness" is commonly considered to be one of these attributes of God. By speaking of the righteousness of God in these terms, the idea is conveyed that "righteousness" is a designation of a *quality* within God, a designation of the very core and essence of his being and nature. Is that what Paul means when he uses the term? Generally, the answer to that question has been "yes." The logical consequence of that understanding of the righteousness of God for the human predicament and for our redemption has been as follows: Since God is perfect righteousness, we can only stand in his presence when we become perfectly righteous. Therefore, something must be done about us. And since, according to Paul, we are sinners and cannot become righteous before God no matter how hard we try, there is only one option: God himself has to intervene and change us. How does that happen?

Operating with the idea that righteousness is a quality of God, one line of interpretation has held that "the righteousness of God revealed in faith" designates our righteousness, given to us by God and valid before God. This is what is meant by the terms *infused* or *imparted* righteousness. This means that on the basis of our response to Christ in faith, God somehow takes of his own righteousness, or Christ's righteousness, and pours it into our very being. The idea is that we are *given a new core*, that we are transformed at the very center of our being, that our own quality of *unrighteousness* is displaced by God's *righteousness*. The result of such an understanding of the salvation event is a frustrating dilemma: In terms of our problem—namely, the gap between what we affirm about our Christian existence and what we actually are—a question is raised as to the relationship between our "new core" and our actual living. If the act of justification transforms us at the center of our very beings from where our lives are motivated, driven, and oriented, then why is so much of our living out of joint, why is there such a gap between what we are and what we ought to be? We shall return to that problem later.

A second line of interpretation, which derives from the basic idea that "righteousness" designates primarily a quality within the nature of God, has held that Paul thinks of a court of law when he speaks of the righteousness of God and the justification of humankind. The picture conveyed is something like the following: Humankind stands in the dock, guilty before God, the Judge. The sentence of condemnation is about to be pronounced. But, on the basis of Jesus' self-giving on the cross, the sentence of condemnation is transformed into a pronouncement of acquittal. This means that "God's righteousness" is conveyed to the sinner by virtue of a *declaration*. The guilty, unrighteous sinner is *declared to be righteous as if he or she actually were that*. The result of this interpretation of the salvation event is no less problematic than the one discussed above. For how are we to understand the relationship between such a "declaration" and the actuality of our Christian existence? Indeed, why should God *declare* anything? To whom does he declare it? Is he answerable to anything or anyone outside himself? This view involves us in holding that God pronounces persons to be righteous when in reality they are nothing of the sort. Sanday and Headlam, in their commentary on Romans, aptly describe this state of affairs as legal "fiction."[1]

The difficulty encountered in both of the above understandings of Paul's use of the concept "righteousness of God" is due to the fact that: (1) the term "righteousness" is used in its ordinary sense, and (2) God is thought to need some kind of righteousness from a person before salvation can be granted. And since actual righteousness is impossible, it must be either *imparted* or *imputed*. As Norman Snaith has rightly pointed out, there are two errors here. One is that we have not really emancipated ourselves from that very doctrine which Paul spent most of his life combatting— namely, that salvation is somehow tied to righteousness. The other is that the term "righteousness" is interpreted as though there were never any Old Testament.[2] Let us therefore turn to the background of the concept of righteousness to gain a clearer perception of what it might have meant for Paul.

Our ordinary understanding of the term righteousness is very much in line with its common Greek meaning. For the ancient Greeks, righteousness and justice were very cold, impartial things. They felt that there was an absolute standard of *rightness* to which both persons and gods must conform. A person was considered to be righteous if he or she satisfied ordinary legal demands, lived the virtuous, moral life, and fulfilled the prescribed civic duties. Now, since Paul used this Greek term in writing to the church in the Hellenistic world, it has often been assumed that he used it on their terms, as something which denotes a *personal, ethical quality*. But it must be remembered that a goodly number of the recipients of

Paul's letters were either Diaspora Jews or God-fearers[3] and that Paul assumes almost everywhere a good working knowledge of the Old Testament. Again, Paul was a Hebrew born of Hebrews (Philippians 3:5-6), saturated with a knowledge of the Old Testament, having been educated at the feet of Gamaliel, one of the renowned rabbinic teachers of the first century.[4] It is thus important to gain an appreciation of Paul's heritage and to recover the roots of his understanding concerning the "righteousness of God."

In the Old Testament, "righteousness" is basically a *relational* concept which designates the *action of partners* in keeping with the *covenant relationship*. It does not denote primarily a personal, ethical quality, but a relationship which is characterized by faithfulness. Thus, *God's faithful action* in reference to his covenant people is designated as "righteous." Let us briefly look at several selected passages from the Old Testament which clearly express these Hebrew ideas.

Speaking of the hope of Israel and of the One who would come forth out of the Davidic line, Isaiah characterizes him with these words (all italics in quotations to follow added by author):

> *Righteousness* shall be the
> girdle of his waist,
> and *faithfulness* the girdle
> of his loins.
> (Isaiah 11:5)

These lines are a beautiful example of a trademark of Hebrew poetry, namely, "parallelism." That is, the writer expresses one idea in two or more ways. The affirmation of the first pair of lines (in 11:5) is reaffirmed and underlined by being expressed in different words in the second pair of lines. Thus, *righteousness* is *synonymous* with *faithfulness*.

In Isaiah 16:5, another term is introduced which is at the core of Israel's faith concerning God's acts on its behalf:

> . . . a throne will be established
> in *steadfast love*
> and on it will sit in *faithfulness*
> in the tent of David
> one who judges and seeks justice
> and is swift to do *righteousness*.

Here, the terms *steadfast love* and *faithfulness* are closely associated with the word *righteousness*. The context of these lines shows that the prophet is speaking about a time when oppression and destruction have come to an end, and the situation will be characterized by one sitting on the throne of David who "does righteousness," i.e., who is present in steadfast love and faithfulness.

That these ideas are closely tied into the Hebraic understanding of God's saving action is demonstrated by the passage in Isaiah 26:1-3:

> . . . "We have a strong city;
>   he sets up *salvation*
>   as walls and bulwarks.
> Open the gates,
>   that the *righteous nation* which
>   *keeps faith*
>   may enter in.
> Thou dost keep him in perfect peace,
>   whose mind is stayed on thee,
>   because he *trusts* in thee."

Salvation is a reality for the "righteous nation," i.e., for those who "keep faith" with God, who are related to him in "trust." The "righteous nation" is not so much a people who are ethically, morally above reproach, but rather a people who recognize their dependence upon the One who is the giver of life and live before him in trust and faithfulness.

The psalmist of Psalm 5 speaks apparently out of a difficult and threatening situation when he utters these words:

> But I through the abundance of thy
>   *steadfast love*
>   will enter thy house,
> I will worship toward thy holy temple
>   in the fear of thee.
> Lead me, O Lord, in thy *righteousness*
>   because of my enemies;
>   make thy way straight before me.
>
>   (Psalm 5:7-8)

In the hour of despair, the psalmist recognizes that only God's steadfast love will restore him to God's presence (that is what "entering God's house" means), and, in appealing for that divine intervention, he asks to be led out of the despairing situation by God's righteousness. The psalmist of Psalm 85 expresses a similar sentiment in even more striking terms:

> Show us thy *steadfast love*, O Lord,
>   and grant us *thy salvation*.
> *Steadfast love* and *faithfulness*
>   will meet;

> *righteousness* and *peace* will kiss
>   each other.
> *Faithfulness* will spring up
>   from the ground,
> and *righteousness* will look down
>   from the sky.
> *Righteousness* will go before him,
>   and make his footsteps a way.
>   (Psalm 85:7, 10, 11, 13)

This psalm comes from the situation of Israel after the Exile. The people have been restored to their land (v. 1) and have seen this as a sign of God's forgiveness (vv. 2-3). Yet there is the recognition that all is not as it should be, that real joy does not characterize the new situation (vv. 4-6). And so the psalmist cries out for the full manifestation of God's steadfast love which will result in salvation. In his prayer he apparently receives God's assurance (vv. 8-9), and so he concludes with a doxology in which God's redeeming intervention is described variously and interchangeably with the terms *steadfast love, righteousness, faithfulness,* and *peace.* It is apparent that "righteousness" has nothing to do here with morality or ethics or virtue—though these are everywhere expected to be the outgrowth of the relation with God—but that it is a term which has to do with *God's action toward his creation.*

In a praise of God as the Creator, we find the following lines:

> Thou hast a mighty arm;
>   strong is thy hand,
>   high thy right hand.
> *Righteousness* and *justice* are
>   the foundation of thy throne;
>   *steadfast love* and *faithfulness*
>   go before thee.
>   (Psalm 89:13-14)

As in Isaiah 11:5, we have here another beautiful example of Hebrew poetry with its parallel structure. The terms *righteousness* and *justice* are clearly used in synonymous parallelism with the terms *steadfast love* and *faithfulness.* From an affirmation about God's activity as Creator (vv. 5-12), which is summarized in verse 13, the psalmist moves to a statement about the Creator's relationship to his people (14-18). He does not speculate as to the nature of this God. Thus, the terms *righteousness* and *justice* are not abstract nouns, descriptive of God's nature; they are what may be called "action words." Defined by *steadfast love* and *faithfulness,* they speak of God's saving relationship toward Israel. This saving relationship is strikingly expressed in the praise of Psalm 98:2-3, where the words *righteousness, faithfulness,* and *steadfast love* are again used interchangeably to denote the content of God's redeeming action:

> The LORD has made known his *salvation;*
>   he has revealed his *righteousness*
>   in the sight of the nations.
> He has remembered his *steadfast love*
>   and *faithfulness*
>   to the house of Israel.
> All the ends of the earth have seen
>   the salvation of our God.
>   (author's translation)[5]

From the above discussion, it should be clear that in the context of Israel's relationship with God, his *activity*, that is, his merciful, redeeming, restoring, upholding action, is described as "God's righteousness." Therefore, "to justify" persons did not mean to pronounce them or to find them to be righteous, but to secure their vindication, to save them from their oppressors, to redeem them from difficult and threatening situations. For this way of thinking and believing, "righteousness" is identical with "saving deed," with salvation.

Nor was such thinking restricted to the religious expression of Israel as preserved in the Old Testament Scriptures. There is a plentiful amount of evidence in the Jewish literature produced in the period between the Testaments that such ways of speaking about God's intervention in human history and human lives continued, despite the increasing influx of Greek modes of thought. This is particularly true of some of the literary remains recovered from the caves at Qumran, commonly known as the Dead Sea Scrolls. The reader may be surprised to find that some expressions in the "Hymns" from Qumran seem to form a connecting bridge between Old Testament affirmations about the righteousness of God and the Pauline statements. We shall cite several examples here.

In Hymn IV, the writer reflects on his weakness and impotence before God:

> Righteousness, I know, is not of man,
>   nor is perfection of way of the son of man:
> to the Most High God belong all righteous deeds.
> The way of man is not established
>   except by the spirit which God created for him
>   to make perfect a way for the children of men. . . .

> I lean on Thy grace
> > and the multitude of Thy mercies,
> for Thou wilt pardon iniquity,
> > and through Thy righteousness
> [Thou wilt purify man] of his sin.[6]

The righteousness of God is here interpreted in terms of *grace* and *mercy*. God's righteous deeds, his saving intervention, is that which restores persons to relationship with God.

In a hymn of thanksgiving, the writer says:

> I [will bring forth] a reply of the tongue
> > to recount Thy righteous deeds. . . .

The context shows that he is thinking of God's mighty *saving deeds* on behalf of Israel. Then he goes on to apply that knowledge to his own situation:

> [For] Thine, Thine is righteousness. . . .
> [According to] Thy righteousness,
> > let [Thy servant] be redeemed. . . .
> > > > > (Hymn XVII)[7]

In these lines it is unequivocally clear that the hymn-writer understands God's saving intervention in his own life in analogy to God's saving deeds on behalf of Israel and speaks of both in terms of "God's righteousness."

Many more such passages could be cited, but we shall conclude our look at this background material by citing a striking passage from Hymn XIV:

> Thou wilt blot out all wickedness . . . for ever,
> > and *Thy righteousness shall be revealed*
> before the eyes of all Thy creatures.[8]
> > > > > (Italics added)

The italicized phrase can hardly fail to evoke a surprising recognition. Is it possible that Paul had before his mind's eye this passage from Qumran? We do not know if Paul ever had, before or after the Damascus road experience, any contact with the Qumran covenanters. In any case, his affirmation in Romans 1:17 that "the righteousness of God is revealed" answers the longing and hope expressed by the hymn-writer in the Judean hills. There we have *future expectation:* "Thy righteousness *shall be* revealed"; in Paul we have *present realization:* "God's righteousness *is revealed.*"

With the foregoing background study in mind, let us now proceed to a look at the texts in Romans where the phrase "the righteousness of God" appears. We begin with an overview of the central thrust of Paul's argument before we treat the specific texts.

For Paul, the "unrighteousness" of humankind (Romans 1:18; 2:8; 3:5)[9] is the result of *disobedience,* or better, the condition of disobedience, whether that be—

1. persons in general, who refuse to acknowledge God (1:28) within the *Creator-creature relationship,* obeying unrighteousness and disobeying truth (2:8), or

2. the Jew, who refuses to acknowledge God within the *covenant relationship,* who disobeys and thus is unfaithful (3:3; 10:21).

Thus, the *unrighteousness* of persons does not denote primarily an ethical quality or disposition within persons. This would be a general Greek conception which seems to be far from Paul's thought. Rather, it denotes the state of a particular relationship. That is, persons are unrighteous when their relationship with God is severed, when they assert their independence over against God, when they refuse to accept their limitations and wish to reject their creatureliness, when they boast of their own achievements, when they seek to establish their own rightness before God.

The striking picture which Genesis 2 paints of the fall of Adam — who is really the representative, typical human being—is an apt illustration of the break within the Creator-creature relationship. This typical human being is not rejected by God because of a lapse of moral behavior; he is not found to be "unrighteous" in the ordinary meaning of that word. No, the divine-human relationship is severed because persons refuse to accept their limitation and reject their dependence. This stance is powerfully rendered in the poem *Invictus* by William Ernest Henley:

> Out of the night that covers me,
>   Black as the Pit from pole to pole,
> I thank whatever gods may be
>   For my unconquerable soul.
>
> In the fell clutch of circumstance
>   I have not winced nor cried aloud.
> Under the bludgeonings of chance
>   My head is bloody, but unbowed.
>
> Beyond this place of wrath and tears
>   Looms but the Horror of the shade,
> And yet the menace of the years
>   Finds, and shall find, me unafraid.
>
> It matters not how strait the gate,
>   How charged with punishments the scroll,
> I am the master of my fate;
>   I am the captain of my soul.[10]

In Romans 1:18-32, Paul describes the depth of corruption and degradation into which persons can sink as a result of such a stance of independence.

The break within the covenant relationship may be illustrated from the Gospels' account of the young ruler who came to Jesus with the question concerning eternal life (Mark 10:17-22 and parallels). Jesus proceeded to conduct a little examination concerning the man's relationship to the law. That is, he asked him about his ethics, his morality, his life-style. Surprisingly, the man passed the test with flying colors. With a certain air of pious self-righteousness, he proclaimed his moral uprightness: "All these I have observed from my youth!" There is no reason to believe that he was telling a lie. In fact, the text tells us that Jesus looked upon him and loved him. He probably was a very "righteous" individual from the point of view of morality. But the whole point of the text is that he was empty nonetheless; he was seeking; he was not whole. His search is an apt illustration of St. Augustine's "restlessness of soul":

> O Lord . . . thou hast formed us for Thyself
> And our hearts are restless till they find rest in Thee.[11]

For the man in the Gospel story, the restlessness continues, for he is unwilling, ultimately, to yield his independence and to live his life in dependence upon the Giver of life.

Paul's own life, in retrospect, was for him a poignant example of a break within the covenant relationship. He tells us unequivocally that, as far as his legal righteousness was concerned, he was blameless (Philippians 3:6). But his Damascus road experience and his continuing confrontation with Christ convinced him that even at its highest, his morality and piety were not worth as much as a heap of garbage (Philippians 3:7-9).

In light then of this understanding of the "unrighteousness" of humankind as a severed relationship, the question which Paul seeks to answer in Romans is this: How is this unrighteousness removed? That is, how are persons restored to the proper relationship with God and what must characterize that relationship? If the relationship which bears the caption "unrighteous" is characterized by *disobedience,* then the restored relationship must be characterized by *obedience.* And this is exactly Paul's announced purpose for his mission of proclaiming the gospel: to bring about the *obedience of faith* (Romans 1:5; 16:26). Paul is concerned to lead his fellow earthlings to the place where, in response to the Good News of God's intervention in the chaos of human existence, they find themselves restored to the situation in which through faithful obedience they respond to the Creator. That, for Paul, is true freedom. For the freedom of the creature consists, not in independence, in self-assertion, but in a life which is lived out within the purposes of the Creator for his creatures. It is in that sense that Jesus was the *true human being;* it is in that sense that he was truly free, though he was the servant par excellence—he lived his life out fully within the purposes of God.

We see then that Paul's thinking about righteousness moves within the context of a *relational-reality,* as opposed to an *essential reality* (imparted righteousness) or a *judicial reality* (declared righteousness). Our faithlessness, our negative response within this relationship is designated as "unrighteousness." While God's action in the context of this relationship is characterized by the opposite: God is faithful to his creation/covenant relationship (3:3f), his action is "righteous" (3:26), and it is this action in response to his rebellious creation which Paul therefore calls "the righteousness of God." This term designates that *activity of God* which *restores the severed relationship.* "Righteousness" in this context is thus not an attribute of God, but is the term which designates his *forgiving* and *redemptive intervention* in the world by means of the Christ event. The restored relationship is one in which God is recognized as Creator and Lord by a creature who in freedom is able to respond obediently.

An examination of the passages where the phrase "the righteousness of God" appears in Romans (1:17; 3:5; 3:21-26; 10:3) seems to support the overall interpretation suggested above.

Romans 1:16-17

In order to get at the precise significance of these thematic verses, we need to look at each phrase to determine its specific meaning. For that purpose we propose here an expanded translation from the Greek text:

> I am not ashamed of the Good News concerning the Christ event, for this event is the power of God that results in salvation for everyone who believes. . . . For in that event God's restoring love has become concrete reality in the context of the life of faith . . . (author's translation).

For Paul, the "power of God" does not reside in the words of the proclamation as such. The content of the gospel (literally, "good news") is precisely defined in the opening words of the epistle as "the [good news] concerning his Son" (1:3). Then, in capsule form, the central message of the early church concerning Jesus' Davidic descent, his resurrection, and his present lordship are given (1:3-5). For Paul, then, the redemptive power of God is not in the description of the event, but in the event itself. It is that event which brings salvation for everyone "who believes." The translation of the RSV—"who has faith"—misses something of the Pauline dynamic expressed in the use of the present tense which indicates a *continuing* reality. After the affirmation of verse 16, it is really necessary to ask the hypothetical question: "*Why* is Paul not ashamed of the proclamation of that event, and *how* is it the power of God?" Paul's answer follows in verse 17. It is instructive to compare the expanded translation given above with the RSV's translation: "For in it the righteousness of God is revealed through faith for faith. . . . " The phrase "is revealed" points to a *concrete historical manifestation,* an appearing, a presence. When Paul says in the following verse (18) that the "wrath of God is revealed," he means that the wrath of God is manifesting itself presently in the various degradations and corruptions that he describes so forcefully in verses 18-32. Paul uses the same words to describe the final, historical in-breaking of God into the world through the return of Christ (1 Corinthians 1:7; 2 Thessalonians 1:7; cf. Romans 2:5; 8:19; 1 Corinthians 2:10). The phrase "through faith for faith" indicates a progression and designates the life of faith. It is within the continuing reality of the life of faith that the reality of the power of God unto salvation is apprehended and experienced. This is not a once-for-all experience limited to the beginning of Christian existence. Paul is not ashamed of the Christ event, because he has encountered and continues to encounter the transforming power of it in the context of his life.

To say that "righteousness of God" in this context speaks about a quality of God, imparted to us as human beings, or about a judicial declaration, so that we can stand "righteous" before God, simply misses the thrust of Paul's concern. There is no thought here of a transference of a quality from God to us; nor does Paul here use the imagery of a court of law, where God acts as Judge, dispensing justice. Rather, Paul is talking about an *act of God* which *only in faith* is seen and experienced as God's restoring love.

Romans 3:5

> But if our wickedness [unrighteousness] serves to show the justice [righteousness] of God, what shall we say? . . .

This RSV translation is not a happy one, for it introduces the idea of moral corruption and justice from the outset. Such a concept does not take into consideration the fact that, for Paul, moral failure and alienation from God are not necessarily related, as we demonstrated earlier. It is better to preserve the direct relationship between the Greek words which the RSV translates with "wickedness" and "justice," and translate as follows: "But if our unrighteousness demonstrates God's righteousness, what shall we say?" What Paul brings to expression in these lines is really a repetition of the matter already introduced in the preceding verses: "What if some were unfaithful? Does their faithlessness nullify the faithfulness of God? . . ." The righteousness of God is directly parallel to the faithfulness of God, and both stand directly over against the unrighteousness of humankind and the faithlessness of humankind. This parallel recalls what we found about the close correspondence between "faithfulness" and "righteousness" in the Old Testament. In 3:3, the contrast is between the covenant partners, God and Israel, describing their respective action in respect to that relationship. In 3:5, on the other hand, the contrast is between the Creator, the ruler of the cosmos, and the creature, describing their actions in respect to the Creator-creature relationship. Humankind's end of the relationship is characterized by "unrighteousness," God's by "righteousness." This *relational* interpretation is supported by the quotation from the Psalms given in 3:10f.

> "None is righteous, no, not one;
> no one understands, no one seeks for God.
> All have turned aside. . . ."

Here, the phrase "none is righteous" does not mean, primarily, that no one is morally upright. It means, rather, that "no one is rightly related to God." The parallel phrase, "all have turned aside," underlines such an understanding.

Romans 3:21-26

Again, we offer an expanded translation of verses 21-22 for the sake of clarity and precision: "But now [in contrast to that faithlessness of men which breaks the divine-human relationship] God's restoring love has broken into our history . . ." (author's translation). What has been manifested, what has broken into our history, is *God's forgiving, restoring action* on behalf of his creation. Verse 22 simply gives the instrument by means of which this "righteousness of God" has broken into human history: "It [the 'righteousness of God'] touches us by way of faith in Christ, and continues to touch us in the life of faith" (author's translation).

Now, in what sense does the event of Christ manifest the restoring love of God? This question is answered in verses 24f. It is through the event of Christ that humankind's rebellion is forgiven, and *forgiveness restores a broken relationship.* Because this is purely the act of God, Paul calls it a gift. And because a gift is meaningless unless accepted and appropriated, it must be "received by faith."

The result of this entire redemption is the justification of humankind (26f) or better, the *setting right* of humankind. There is nothing here at all about a transformation of our essence, nor a simple declaration: "In my sight you are now righteous." What we have instead is a restoration to the divine-human relationship. This restoration of rebellious humans demonstrates the righteousness of God (3:25), i.e., the faithfulness and love of God toward his creation. How so? Because in spite of the world's rebellion, he acts for its restoration.

Romans 10:3

In this passage it becomes decisively clear that for Paul, "the righteousness of God" is a term which designates the present manifestation of God's relationship-restoring intervention in human history. Israel, because it attempted to establish its own righteousness—i.e., its own position before God—fatefully missed the coming of God's righteousness in the Christ event—i.e., God's powerful intervention on behalf of humankind. That the term "God's righteousness" denotes this redemptive activity is established in the last part of verse 3: Israel "did not submit" to this righteousness, that is, to this way of God with his world. For to submit means to acknowledge one's severed relationship with God and to confess to the lordship of Christ (10:7). This, Israel refused to do.

Thus, for Paul, to submit to God's righteousness means to submit to his salvation-creating coming in the Christ event. Such submission ushers us into a restored Creator-creature relationship in which God is Lord and in which we in *joyful obedience* recognize our dependence upon our Creator.

In light of the foregoing considerations on the meaning of the concept "the righteousness of God," what does it mean when Paul speaks of God as the one who "justifies" the ungodly, i.e., those who are out of relation with God (Romans 4:5; 3:24, 26, 28, 30)? It means that they are *reclaimed* (Romans 5:8), that they are *reconciled* (2 Corinthians 5:18-19), that they are *restored* to the proper Creator-creature relationship. It is clear from 5:1 that justification *equals* peace with God; and peace with God is a relationship where enmity is gone.

Having done this somewhat demanding groundwork of interpretation, it is now our task briefly to summarize our findings and to indicate what all of this means for our understanding of the nature of Christian existence.

1. *The salvation event, both in terms of its inception and in terms of its continuation, does not result in a new person, but in a new situation.* The gap between, on the one hand, the affirmation "the old has passed away" and, on the other, the continuing struggle with the old, is therefore not to be explained by a conflict between a "new core" within us and the "old self." It is rather due to the fact that as individuals who have been reclaimed by God, we are confronted by the old and the new and are faced with the need to decide.

The matter may be stated in yet another way: Christian existence is characterized by a *change of lordship,* not by a change within our inmost being. Alteration of our moral-ethical-spiritual core would mean either of two things: (1) First, it would mean that all our actions are now in conformity with the divine purposes for us. Since our experience of daily reality belies that, the question of the relationship between the new core and our daily living remains unanswered, indeed, inexplicable. (2) Alternately, transformation of the core of our being would mean that God's redemptive activity is restricted to only a portion of our being. In such a case, "I," as a concrete, historical being, would not be the object of God's love and forgiveness at all, but only some indefinable, abstract *part* of the "I" which, for want of better terms, we generally designate with the words "soul" or "spirit." But the entire New Testament literally cries out against such a limited view of redemption. Some such view of the nature of salvation was in fact current in the young church at Corinth, and Paul decisively rejected it. Various Hellenistic philosophies and religions taught the redemption and liberation of the human soul. Over against that stream of thought, the New Testament dares to proclaim the redemption and liberation of *persons.* The Gospel of John expresses that idea beautifully when it emphasizes the presence of eternity in the midst of time: "He who believes has eternal life" (John 6:47).

If the salvation event brings about a change of lordship, then we are dealing with a new situation, insofar as we are now confronted by the need to respond with the totality of our lives to this lordship. If Christian existence is characterized by a change of lordship, then we are existing in a situation in which we are called upon to bring the mind of Christ to bear upon the concrete demands of daily living. If the salvation event sets us free for a new kind of existence, then we continually stand at the crossroads where we must decide between allegiance to this new Lord who forgives our rebelliousness or to the various "gods and lords" which beckon us, which are, indeed, often our own creations, and at whose altars we are always tempted to serve. In subsequent chapters, we shall have the opportunity to speak about this crossroads existence in more detail.

2. *The salvation event, i.e., justification, is liberation for a new possibility.* From the actuality of the old disobedience the Christian has moved into the possibility of the new obedience. Christian existence is therefore not to be understood as a new actuality, but as a new possibility.

A second look at the passage from 2 Corinthians 5:17, quoted in the Introduction, would be helpful for clarification at this point. We have already discussed the difficulty with which this Pauline affirmation concerning the "new creation" confronts the serious and sensitive Christian who constantly recognizes the presence of the old together with the new. The difficulty arises basically from a misunderstanding of the Pauline intention. What, we must ask, is Paul expressing here? In what sense are Christians "new creations"?

An instructive perspective comes to light when Paul's affirmation is seen against the backdrop of Israel's prophetic hope, in which Paul certainly participated. One of the cardinal precepts of the prophetic hope was the belief that the *end of time* was going to be like the *beginning of time.* (The Germans can express that in a precise word-play equation: *Endzeit=Urzeit;* an English equivalent would be: final period=primal period.) When the prophets spoke about the expectation of God's final coming and reign in human history, they frequently described that time in imagery associated in the Old Testament with paradise and the original creation. That is, the end time was understood to correspond in its characteristics to the beginning of time. A new creation was going to emerge out of the old. Isaiah's picture of the return of paradise is a striking example of this strain in the prophetic expectation:

> The wolf shall dwell with the lamb,
>> and the leopard shall lie down with the kid,
> and the calf and the lion and the fatling together,
>> and a little child shall lead them.
>
> (Isaiah 11:6)

Again, it is Isaiah who speaks of the time of salvation in terms of a paradisical condition of peace. It is a vision of such grandeur and of such abiding and universal human appeal that its words were inscribed at the base of a sculpture at the United Nations Plaza in New York:

> . . . they shall beat their swords into ploughshares,
>> and their spears into pruning hooks;
> nation shall not lift up sword against nation,
>> neither shall they learn war any more.
>
> (Isaiah 2:4)

Now for Paul, the end of time had dawned upon a broken world. The end of the ages had broken into the old age. The world was a new world insofar as it had encountered the Creator in the event of Christ. The person "in Christ" was part of a new humanity, created in Christ Jesus for a new kind of existence. That is to say, as Adam, the typical human being, stood before the Creator in radical freedom, so the new person in Christ stands before the Creator in radical freedom. The situation of Adam before the Fall has been re-created; it is in that sense, and only in that sense, that the Christian is a "new creation." As Adam was faced with the decision either to give allegiance to God the Creator or to create his own gods and give allegiance to them, so the new-creation person is faced with the same decision. As Adam lived with the possibility of either dependence upon his Creator or independence from him, so the new-creation person exists within that possibility. As Adam could either exist in fellowship with his Maker or hide from him among the trees, so the new-creation person can either live in trust with his Maker or make jungles in which to hide from him.

The salvation event *does not guarantee* the former of these alternatives. What it does do is to grasp persons from the chaos of their enslavements and bondages, from the death-grips of the old impossibility, and transfers them into the freedom and light of a new possibility. To be a new creation is to live out of that new possibility and freedom in joyful response to the Creator and to our fellow creatures.

3. The recognition that justification places the Christian in the situation of a new possibility *ought to lead to the celebration and affirmation of tension and process and change.*

We have come through a period in our recent history in which relativity in almost all areas of life has been on the throne. There has been a rejection or suppression of anything which smacked of absolutes, of controls, of systems, and of structures. An example of that was the early hippie movement and the subsequent emergence of the various countercultures. These were characterized by an anti-institutionalism, the rejection of authority, the "do-your-own-thing" syndrome. In the world of education, the ideas of Thomas Dewey carried the day, emphasizing freedom of expression and rejection of formal structures and authoritative discipline. In the world of morality and social relationships, we witnessed the emergence of "situation ethics," which in many ways served to cast a mantle of respectability and philosophical acceptability around the shoulders of the increasingly influential "Hollywood mentality" and "Playboy philosophy."

This "era of relativity and flux" has had, for many, many persons, an unsettling and unnerving impact. Traditional anchors, norms, and values by which they stabilized, ordered, and oriented their lives seemed to be disintegrating. Such a mood of uncertainty has led gradually to a backlash, so that the pendulum in many quarters has swung to the other extreme. Our more recent history seems to be characterized by a withdrawal from relativity into absolutes, into clearly defined securities, into authoritative structures which leave little room for uncertainties.

Such retrenchment has not been without influence in the arena of the church. Dean Kelley documents this influence in his book, *Why Conservative Churches are Growing.*[12] Among the various causes which he subjects to critical analysis, description, and evaluation, one is that these churches often provide a clearly defined system of beliefs and "correct" doctrinal formulations, as well as precise codes of morality and conduct. In the midst of the relativity and flux and unsettling events of life, persons are seeking for, and are provided with, secure boundaries within which to live. Again, the immense popularity and success of Bill Gothard's "Institute for Basic Youth Conflicts" shows that a rigorous authoritarian system, which provides most, if not all, the answers for everyday living, gives to both youth and parents an attractive escape hatch from uncertainty into security. On the one hand are youth who have grown up in an era of permissiveness. They have not been provided with a compass for life. And so they grasp the lifeline of discipline and structure. On the other hand are parents who have been battered by the "generation gap" syndrome. They have barely held their heads above the water during the era of the youth rebellion. So now they gratefully and desperately cling to the rescue boat whose captain offers them the possibility of regaining their self-worth and a measure of control over their broken and often chaotic family situations.

It can hardly be doubted that the swing of the pendulum away from the era of relativity was not only inevitable, but a somewhat healthy antidote. And yet a flag of caution must be raised, for it is likely that the benefits of the swing into clearly defined securities are primarily of short-term duration. As Aristotle recognized over two millenia ago, there is such a thing as a "golden mean" between two extremes. In terms of our concern, the *codification of Christian existence* is one such extreme. It stands over against another extreme: a Christian existence which rejects all boundaries and all absolutes and is constantly threatened by dissolution into a wishy-washy, sentimental love ethic. The "golden mean" between these extremes is *responsible existence in faith under the lordship of Christ.* To remove the tensions within Christian existence is to pave the way toward personal stagnation and death.

We must never forget the Pauline dynamic of the movement between the "already" and the "not-yet." Christian existence is seeing through a smoked glass and experiencing through limited perception (1 Corinthians 13:12). The answers are not all in, and the architects of biblical absolutism who hand down authoritative answers for any and all situations have simply not understood the dynamic of the biblical witness to God's way with his creation! It is not accidental that the New Testament describes Christians as the new Israel; but not Israel as it existed in the Promised Land, rather Israel as it was on the move between Egypt and the Promised Land (1 Corinthians 10:1-13). Christians, as was Israel, are the wandering people of God. Christian existence is a pilgrim existence in the desert of decision, lived out between the magnetic poles of "Egypt" and the "Promised Land," between the attractions of the "City of Man" and the "City of God." It is far better, and healthier, to affirm that tension and to celebrate it than to deny and suppress it. The former has within it the possibility of maturation and growth of the Christian person; the latter leads to infantilism and possibly to the destruction of one's personhood.

I never tire of telling my students that it is not wrong, or un-

Christian, to think heretically when searching for truth. Much of the scriptural witness to the reality of God and to the meaning of that reality for our lives is the result of dialogue between those who gave that witness and their understanding of the revelation of God. Our own encounter with God must be no less. We must be willing to wrestle with God, to ask the hard questions, to reexamine traditional beliefs and understandings. Dr. Charles Boddie, in a recent commencement address at Northern Baptist Theological Seminary, emphasized the absolute necessity of "the question mark in Christian syntax," for without it, the syntax of Christian existence is incomplete. Only the interrogative, the question mark, provides the possibility for expansion and growth.

4. *The new situation into which we are ushered by the salvation event places upon us the obligation of participation.* In the same context in which Paul affirms that in Christ we have become new creations (2 Corinthians 5:17), he also speaks about becoming involved in the ministry of reconciliation (vv. 18-20). Then he climaxes that discussion with the claim that the purpose of the Christ event was "that in him we might become the righteousness of God" (v. 21). What is Paul saying here? Let us recall our understanding of the righteousness of God as God's relation-restoring intervention in the midst of human history. Now in the context of an appeal to become participants in the ministry of reconciliation, Paul speaks about Christians as becoming the righteousness of God. Thus, to become the righteousness of God means to become incarnations of his restoring love in the midst of our world.

As those who exist on the threshold of the new possibility, and recognize both the freedom and responsibility of that kind of existence, we must increasingly be and become mediators of God's reconciling, forgiving, and healing love in the midst of our broken and confused world.

Questions for Discussion and Reflection

1. God's act of righteousness means our acceptance into a life-giving relationship. What implications does that have for our self-understanding?

2. What does it mean to be a "new creation"? Think of ways in which such an understanding can affect moral decisions.

3. What are the characteristic elements of "God's righteousness"? In what ways do these affect our relationship with others?

4. As Christians, we are placed into a situation of freedom where growth is a real possibility. How do we *grow* as Christian persons?

CHAPTER 2

Between the Adamic Humanity and the New Humanity

As we move into this chapter and the rest of the book, let us keep in clear focus the perspective worked out above. Namely, that for Paul, salvation or the in-breaking of God's restoring love in the event of Christ, creates a new situation in which persons are freed for the possibility of a new kind of existence. That perspective is foundational for what will follow in the remaining chapters. The precedent for such a procedure is set by Paul in his Letter to the Romans, where chapters 1–3 are foundational for what follows in the rest of the letter.

In order to get a clear picture of the movement and thrust of Paul's argument, let us take a look at the basic outline of the first few chapters:

1:16-17 announces the theme.

1:18-3:20 sets the stage; here we have a presentation of the human condition—our need.

3:21-31 is the presentation of the eruption of God's restoring love into the broken world by means of the event of Christ.

4:1-25 provides a scriptural proof text for Paul's assertion that God's restoring love does not depend upon human performance.

5:1-11 is pure doxology. Here we have the response which arises out of the experience of God's forgiveness. In the first few chapters, Paul lectured! Here he joins himself to the Christian community in confessional praise: we have peace;

> we are restored to relationship with our Maker; we rejoice;
> we hope; we shall be saved. One can hardly miss the note of
> celebration in these verses.

In view of the development of Paul's thought as briefly sketched above, the passage of 5:12-21 is both a *flashback* and a *flashforward*. It is a flashback in that it reaches back behind 1:18–3:20, which describes the human condition, and asks about the reason for that condition. It is also a flashforward in that it gets at the significance of the event of Jesus for human living.

Thus, Romans 5:12-21 acts as the picturesque presentation of what may be called "the great reversal" (see the diagram below). We have here the turning point of the epistle in that this part catches up in a nutshell what has gone before and lays down the theme of what is to follow. The various tensions on which Paul centers in the rest of the epistle grow out of this basic tension: that the Christian stands in the arena of decision between the Adamic Humanity and the New Humanity. Let us now proceed to an interpretation of that tension.

The key word in Paul's description of the human condition in 1:18–3:20 is the word "sin." This term is picked up again in the opening lines of the passage 5:12-21. What does Paul mean by that term? What is his understanding of the human condition?

The human condition is best summarized in two phrases by Paul: (1) ". . . they did not see fit to acknowledge God . . ." (1:28) and (2) ". . . you . . . rely upon the law [i.e., legalistic religion] and boast of your relation to God" (2:17). That is to say, *sin* is our refusal to accept our creatureliness, to acknowledge our dependence on our

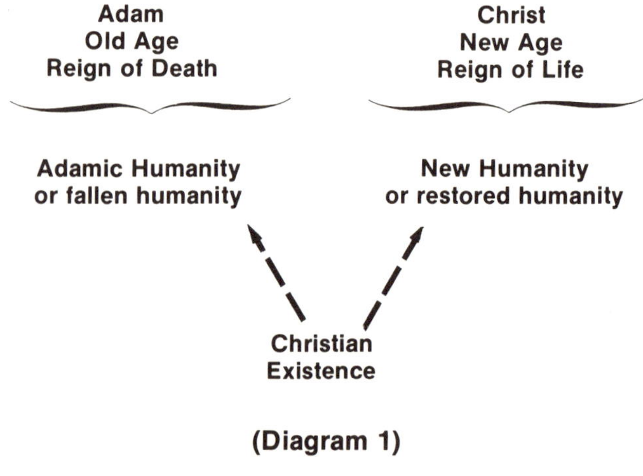

(Diagram 1)

Maker, to recognize our limitations. The affirmation—"we are sinners"—*does not mean*, primarily, that we have moral problems, *but* that, in the deepest and final sense, we are severed from relationship with God and are thus *out of touch with him.*

"Sin" is *not* a thing. We have so often "thingified" sin and have drawn quantitative comparisons between one person's "sin" and that of other persons. Nor is sin a *genetic defect.* This idea, that sin is passed on genetically and thereby becomes the property of each individual through heredity, ultimately led to the puritanical view of sex. In such a view, the sex act is seen as the prime locus of human sinfulness. It is to be tolerated for the purpose of procreation, but its place in God's economy for human wholeness and fulfillment is hardly recognized.

Nor is sin a *perverted inner nature.* The problem with this understanding of sin is that it has divided the individual into a number of separate boxes. It arises from the idea that the Fall resulted in the *perversion of one essential part of our selves.* A number of candidates have been proposed. For some, the perverted part is the *will.* For others, it is the *emotions* or *passions.* For still others, it is human *rationality.* The pervasive mood of anti-intellectualism in some circles of Christians is traceable to some such understanding of humankind. The assumption is that the human mind was affected by the Fall, that, as a result, our reasoning capacity was perverted and depraved, and that the quest of the mind cannot therefore be trusted. But, at the same time, it is almost tacitly assumed, though it is never stated, that the emotions and feelings, our capacity for experiences, have not been affected by the Fall and that these therefore provide a valid index for our spirituality.

It seems clear to me that such an assumption is basically un-Christian: We as *persons* are fallen and stand under the judgment of God. Both our heads and hearts stand under the signature of death. Both are subject to the finiteness and imperfection and limitation of human existence. Both are dust.

The understanding of sin as something inherited and as perverted human nature led the early Roman church into the sacrament of infant baptism. But such a view of sin is not restricted to the Catholic context. When a young child, even before the process of conditioning has begun, acts deliberately against the express command of a parent, the comment can often be heard: "Aha, original sin!" The thought expressed here is that the child, by virtue of an "inherited nature," is predisposed to sin.

This writer is increasingly convinced that such a view is incorrect. Because, from the biblical point of view, the term "sin" designates a particular kind of relationship between the creature and the Creator. And a relationship cannot be inherited; it can only be established or destroyed, affirmed or denied. "Sin" thus understood, namely, as *relational reality,* can express itself in a number of ways:

1. *In wrongdoing* (what we have traditionally labeled "sins"): lying, stealing, murder, immorality, etc. Paul talks about such expressions of humankind's unrelatedness to God in a number of passages (see Romans 1:18f; 1 Corinthians 6:9-10; Colossians 3:5-9). We have really majored in this area, so that "physical" or "external" sins have often been the prime, or even exclusive, target of many Christians' righteous indignation. In the process, other, and often more basic expressions of human unrelatedness to God have been neglected or ignored.

2. *In a righteousness which is boastful and consequently becomes judgmental.* Paul's polemic against legalistic religion in any form fits into this manifestation of humankind's alienation from God. In legalistic righteousness, in a life which depends upon external conformity to a code of conduct, there may not be any evidence of traditional "sins" at all. Yet such a life stands under the caption "sin" just the same. For inevitably it leads to a self-assured righteousness which closes the door to vital, healing relationships.

3. *In emptiness, meaninglessness, anxiety, despair.* Such elements of humankind's condition are caught up in Paul's affirmation in Ephesians 2:12—". . . having no hope and without God in the world." It is the condition of human beings, so aptly brought to focus in St. Augustine's idea, that since humans were created for God, they will be restless until they find rest in a restored relationship. In our "Christianized" civilization, where generally accepted standards of morality and laws which govern social and personal relationships have largely been molded by the Judeo-Christian ethic, we can find any number of persons who live morally upright and good lives, but who are still empty, whose lives are finally without meaning. Such was the condition of the young ruler who asked Jesus how he might enter and experience *LIFE.* In a powerful and penetrating analysis of our recent history, Os Guinness documents these manifestations of human alienation from the Creator's purposes. The title of his work, *The Dust of Death,*[1] strikingly captures much of the mood of our time, which in turn is a reflection of lostness, anxiety, despair.

4. *In walls between us and our brothers and sisters in the human community.* Racial alienation is the most prominent social manifestation of such walls. In the personal arena, the most striking manifestation of such walls is to be seen in the breakdown of relationships between parents and their children, between husbands and wives. It is an open secret that the American family has come upon hard times. Statistics on divorce rates and shattered homes show that the family is everywhere characterized by brokenness, by dissolution, by alienation, by bitterness. It is also no secret that this situation is not confined to those who have no affiliation with the Christian community.

Now the New Testament makes it crystal clear that alienation in social and personal relationships is a direct outgrowth of separation from our Creator. Our relationship with God is tied to our relationship with our fellow creatures:

> Let us love one another; for love is of God, and he who loves is born of God and knows God. He who does not love does not know God; for God is love (1 John 4:7-8).

Human beings were created *in* and *for* relationships. Genesis 1:27 affirms as much when it states that human beings are created, not in individual isolation, but as "male and female," that is, in relationship to one another. Thus, when alienation manifests itself in our intercourse with our fellow human beings, when we are therefore not in touch with God's purposes for us, then we are out of joint and in some respect we are alienated from God our Maker.

5. *In alienation from the created order.* The statements of Paul concerning the created order (Romans 8:19-22) have always been somewhat enigmatic. How ought we to understand such ideas as: "the creation was subjected to futility" or "the creation itself will be set free from its bondage to decay" or "the whole creation has been groaning in travail"? Our recent encounter with the ecological crisis has provided us with a context within which to come to grips with what Paul affirmed so long ago. We are becoming increasingly sensitive to, and aware of, what we have done and are continuing to do to our natural environment. In biblical perspective, humankind's alienation from God is at the root of its misuse and perversion of the environment. Francis Schaeffer treats this manifestation of "sin" quite incisively in his *Pollution and the Death of Man. The Christian View of Ecology.*[2]

We are sinners insofar as we are unrelated to God. The questions raised by that affirmation are: *Why* are we that? *Why* is that our condition? *Why* do we find ourselves in such a dilemma? Paul's attempt to answer such questions is found in Romans 5:12f.

The first verse of that passage is for many *the* proof text *par excellence* for "original sin":

> . . . as sin came into the world through one man and death through sin, and so death spread to all men because all men sinned—

Paraphrased, the "original sin" interpretation sounds like this: "We all stand under the Fall of first man; that is why we are in the mess we are in!" The problem with such a view is that it is wrong, all wrong, for the biblical text does not say that. Paul *does not say* that we sin because Adam sinned. He *does not say* that we die because Adam sinned. What he does say is this: Sin (humankind's alienation from God) entered the stage of history in first man's rebellion. The result of that separation is disintegration and death. But the *universal penetration* of that condition is due to the fact that all persons have sinned; i.e., that all persons become revolutionaries against God.

There is a two-sided perspective here in Paul which must be taken seriously if we wish to understand him adequately. On the one side of this dual perspective is the Hebrew idea of "corporate solidarity,"[3] the recognition that each individual shares in a common humanity. On the other side is the recognition of individual responsibility. By virtue of the former, we are in bondage; by virtue of the latter, we become responsible for participation in that bondage. Let us look at that duality in more detail.

Corporate solidarity. Paul was heir to a tradition concerning the human condition which was deeply rooted in the religious thought of Judaism. That tradition recognized the intimate interdependence of individuals and the good, as well as devastating, effect such human solidarity could have. The Old Testament concept that the sins of parents would have their effect down through several generations reflects the Hebrew idea of corporate solidarity. The immediate background for Paul's statements concerning the relation between first man and the rest of mankind (5:12-21) can be clearly seen in a Jewish work of the first century A.D.

> [Adam] transgressed . . . thou didst appoint death for him and for his descendants. . . .
> For the first Adam, burdened with an evil heart,

transgressed and was overcome, as were also all who were descended from him. Thus the disease became permanent. . . .

(2 Esdras 3:7, 21-22)

O Adam, what have you done? For though it was you who sinned, the fall was not yours alone, but ours also who are your descendants.

(2 Esdras 7:118) [4]

Paul clearly reflects this Jewish understanding in chapter 5. Adam, the typical, representative first human being yields to the temptation to determine his own existence and his own destiny (i.e., he sins). The result of that self-determination is death. Death is the condition of separateness, since the creature apart from the Creator does not have life. Physical death is clearly a part of this picture in the Hebrew-Pauline understanding: separation from the source of life results in decay and disintegration. But both for the Old Testament and for Paul, death is also an existential reality, a real condition of life. Thus, Ezekiel receives a vision of dry bones, that are representative of the failure of Israel to be and remain God's people (Ezekiel 37). Hosea can speak of the resurrection of Israel from the grave of its national downfall (Hosea 6:2). And Paul can speak of Christians as those "who have been brought from death to life" (Romans 6:13). The uniform affirmation of this biblical tradition is that there exists a mysterious relationship between human self-determination and death and between first man's self-determination and our own death (in the most comprehensive sense). We belong to one another, and the condition of one has inevitable repercussions on another.

Sociological and psychological studies have underlined for our time that ancient understanding of human solidarity. We have been shown how heredity, upbringing, and environment play major roles in the formation of our personalities. I am, to a large degree, the product of my world. What I am in the present is a continuation of all that I have assumed—consciously and unconsciously—from my past. Thus, the child raised in an environment with violent models is more likely to be involved in violent behavior than those not raised with such models. The child of psychologically disturbed parents is more likely to become neurotic than the child of mentally healthy parents. The child who grows up in a broken home is less likely to become a whole, healthy person than one raised in a home with genuine love and caring from both parents in a consistent and stable relationship.

All of us are born into a human community that is overshadowed by the cumulative weight of humankind's inhumanity, of oppressive structures, of prejudices, of injustices. We are, all of us, more or less affected by the shadows which these clouds cast onto our motives and orientations, our attitudes and priorities. Tragic examples from the mid-twentieth century abound. There was the Nazi extermination of millions, followed by equally massive Soviet exterminations, where hundreds upon hundreds of generally upright and noncriminal people were drawn into a mass hysteria in which they were able to participate in atrocities unthinkable under other circumstances. There have been the My Lais of Vietnam and other wars, where otherwise quite ethical and good persons were able to become involved in the systematic slaughter of other human beings. These were not premeditated acts for many, but the result of the pervasive and overpowering idea that human beings are expendable. Martin Bell says it cryptically in *The Way of the Wolf*:

> Something like an eternity ago, human beings got all caught up in the illusion that being human is a relatively unimportant sort of proposition.
> . . . In the wake of this basic error there quickly followed the idea that human beings are expendable, which easily degenerated into the proposition that some human beings are expendable. Certain human beings are expendable. Really bad guys are expendable. Guys with low I.Q.'s are expendable. Anyone who disagrees with me is expendable.[5]

Again, there is the pervasive racism in our own society. Persons genuinely unprejudiced in respect to race who move into contexts in which racial strife and enmity are prevalent often expect to find people totally marred by hate and prejudice. What they find instead are quite normal people who have been fitted with blinders concerning race, by social tradition and environment. Those who have come out of that kind of environment recognize the difficulty of shaking off such conditioning.

It is impossible, in the final analysis, to trace the larger manifestations of human evil simply to the isolated acts of single individuals. Human beings are, in a real sense, enslaved to "principalities and powers" which are often nothing more or less than the manifestations of the accumulated weight of the human revolt against the Creator.

> It is becoming more and more obvious, that it is not starvation, not microbes, not cancer but man himself who is mankind's greatest danger.[6]

Individual Responsibility. In the passage of Romans 5:12-21, Paul not only reflects the religious thought of Judaism concerning the fact that we share a common humanity and that we are affected by that interdependence. He also reflects the Jewish tradition that as individuals we are responsible and held accountable for the way we relate to that common humanity.

Already at the time of Ezekiel, a protest was raised against the ancient Hebrew idea that the sins of parents will be brought to bear upon the children and that the children will be held accountable for their parents' transgressions. In Ezekiel 18, the prophet speaks the decisive word of God for individual responsibility:

> "Yet you say, 'Why should not the son suffer for the iniquity of the father?' When the son has done what is lawful . . . he shall surely live. The soul [person][7] that sins shall die. The son shall not suffer for the iniquity of the father . . ." (Ezekiel 18:19-20).

The concept of individual responsibility made itself increasingly felt and is clearly enunciated in Jewish writings close to the time of Paul. In the Wisdom of Solomon, which dates from the first century B.C., the author discusses the presence of evil in the world in clear allusion to Genesis 2:

> Do not invite death by the error
> of your life,
> nor bring on destruction by the
> works of your hands;
> because God did not make death. . . .
> But ungodly men by their words
> and deeds summoned death. . . .
> (1:12-13, 16)
> . . . through the devil's envy
> death entered the world,
> and those who belong to his
> party experience it.
> (2:24)[8]

The parallel between this understanding of individual responsibility and Paul's statement in Romans 5:12 is unmistakable. The same sentiment is voiced quite precisely in a Jewish book of the first century A.D., the Apocalypse of Baruch:

> Adam is therefore not the cause,
> save only of his own soul,
> But each of us has been the
> Adam of his own soul.
> (2 Baruch 54:19)[9]

What Paul, in 5:12, affirms together with his Jewish background is that each person, after Adam, ratifies the rebellion and self-determination of Adam in his or her own experience. It is in that sense that each of us becomes a part of that fateful history which stands under the signature of death. Each individual participates in the Adamic humanity and becomes accountable for that participation. Death marches across the pages of human history because humans in their own individuality have sinned. They have done, in their own existence, what Adam did. And the attempt to determine our own existence, however that may work itself out in everyday living, leads to the condition of being separated from God.

In the face of those voices which have emphasized for our time the sense of human solidarity and interdependence, there is emerging a recovery of the ancient insistence on individual accountability. This is nowhere more striking than in the area of psychotherapy and counseling. In a field which has been dominated by Freudian psychoanalytic theory, with its emphasis on the effects of early childhood experiences and toilet training and a corresponding de-emphasis on the individual's guilt and responsibility,[10] both existential psychotherapy and behavioral approaches, such as William Glasser's concept of "reality therapy," are gaining increasing acceptance.[11] The basic thesis underlying both existential and reality therapeutic approaches stated in simple terms, is this: *you have been shaped by the values, models, and life-styles of your world, but you are nevertheless responsible for the choices you have made, for the ways in which you have responded to and participated in that world.* Indeed, these emphases in humanistic psychology underline individual responsibility as the glue which holds the fabric of human society together. Individual responsibility is absolutely necessary, for the possibility of human community depends upon it. The denial of individual responsibility leads toward chaos. If we reject the mechanistic views of determinism, which hold that each individual's acts are predetermined, then the alternatives are either absolute anarchy or a return to totalitarianism. Neither fit the character of the new creation's individual freedom and responsibility.

Paul, with his background, affirms both human solidarity and individual responsibility. This two-sided reality of the human condition is nowhere more sensitively expressed than in Isaiah 6:5, where the prophet finds himself confronted by God:

> "Woe is me! For I am lost; for I am a man of unclean lips, and I dwell in the midst of a people of unclean lips. . . ."

But if Paul is operating with a dual perspective which recognizes the effect of the cumulative weight of human evil upon each individual but calls for personal accountability, why does he seem to emphasize the inevitable result of Adam's rebellion for all of humankind (5:15-21)? A simple listing of the Pauline statements in this passage is instructive:

> . . . many died through one man's trespass. . . .
> . . . judgment following one trespass brought condemnation. . . .
> . . . because of one man's trespass, death reigned. . . .
> . . . one man's trespass led to condemnation for all men. . . .
> . . . by one man's disobedience, many were made sinners. . . .[12]

All of this sounds quite deterministic! However, side by side with these negative statements are opposing positive ones:

> . . . the grace of that one man Jesus Christ abounded for many. . . .
> . . . one man's act of righteousness leads to acquittal and life for all men. . . .
> . . . by one man's obedience many will be made righteous. . . .[13]

It is important to note that in the diversity of these statements a parallel state of affairs is expressed:

> the many are related to Adam
> as
> the many are related to Christ.

This means that, for Paul, participation in the Adamic Humanity, which is characterized by separation from God, *is like* participation in the New Humanity, which is characterized by restoration to God. According to Paul, how do we become a participant in the New Humanity? The answer to that question fanned the fires of the Protestant Reformation in the sixteenth century: by the response of faith to the demonstration of God's restoring love in the event of Christ. We become participants in the New Humanity by personal commitment, by the decision of faith. Thus, participation in the New Humanity is not the automatic or inevitable result of the Christ event. If that is true, then the parallel structure of the passage under consideration demands that our relationship to the Adamic Humanity must be of the same kind as our relationship to the New Humanity in Christ. What is the nature of that kind of relationship?

A look at 1 Corinthians 15:21-22, which in compact form echoes the substance of Romans 5:15-21, provides us with a clue to the answer.

> For as by a man came death, by a man has come also the resurrection of the dead. For as in Adam all die, so also in Christ shall all be made alive.

For purposes of clarity the correspondence in verse 22 may be given in the following couplet:

> *Just as* those *in Adam* die,
> *so,* those *in Christ* shall be made alive.

The matter expressed here may be stated even more precisely: For those *in Adam*, despite the resurrection of Christ, death has not lost its sting; while for those *in Christ*, despite the prospect of death, it has lost its sting (15:55). The meaning of the little preposition "in" is decisive for an understanding of Paul's thought.

For Paul, human beings can exist variously "in the flesh" (Romans 7:5; 8:8-9) or "in the law" (Romans 3:19; Galatians 3:11) or "in the Spirit" (Romans 8:9; Galatians 3:3; 5:16). What are the realities described by these terms? Paul uses these terms to designate real powers, genuine realities that control persons, that influence and impinge upon their lives. Let us consider some examples that will help to clarify Paul's meaning.

We speak of *materialism* and its power over the lives of people. In the process, we virtually personify that "ism" as if it were some external entity. What we mean, of course, is that materialistic individuals have their lives oriented toward *things* and are consumed by that orientation. *Political ideologies* are similarly realities that cannot be quantified or measured, but they frequently control persons so thoroughly that even the instinct for self-preservation is eliminated. A poignant example of the consuming power of *personal loyalty* emerged during the "Watergate" investigations, when one of President Nixon's advisors testified that he would "walk over his grandmother" for Nixon. Again, the *love* of my wife for me is a reality which impinges on my life, influences my planning, affects my priorities. Thus, to be "in love" means to be influenced by a power which cannot be measured but which is nonetheless very real.

Therefore, to be living life *in the law* means that one is determined by external conformity to a standard of conduct, *even if that standard is the very law of God!* To be living life "in the flesh" does not mean "to be physical" or "to have natural appetites and passions." Rather, to be "in the flesh" means that I live a life with my face turned away from God and turned away from my fellow human beings. To be living life "in the Spirit" is to live a life with my face turned toward God and turned toward my fellow human beings.

With these insights in mind, we are now ready to return to the "in Adam" and "in Christ" formulations. To be "in Adam" means that our lives are determined by the same kind of orientation as the first man's, to be drawn into the history of humankind's alienation, to be an active and sometimes unwitting participant in that history. Conversely, to be "in Christ" means to be determined by the event of Jesus, to be drawn into it, to participate in it by faith, and to be subject to the result of such participation, namely, LIFE.

Insofar as our *total life* is oriented toward conformity with the Adamic Humanity, *we*, as whole persons, are alienated from God. Insofar as our *total life* is oriented toward conformity with the New Humanity, *we*, as whole persons, are related to God.

As Christians we stand at the crossroads of decision between the Adamic Humanity and the New Humanity. And if, as we have maintained, Christian existence is a *new possibility*, then we are *free for* either participation in the one humanity or the other.

How does participation in the Adamic Humanity express itself concretely?

1. By permitting the "dominion of sin" to continue in our lives; by allowing our Christian existence to be undermined by continuing allegiance to realities—gods and lords—which are oriented away from God's purposes for human existence. (That is the subject matter of chapter 3.)

2. By existing in a Christian form of "religious captivity." (That is the subject matter of chapter 4.)

3. By individual self-assertion and ego-directedness. (That is the subject matter of chapter 5).

Participation in the New Humanity is expressed concretely in the opposite of the above: in living under the dominion of life, in Christian freedom, in communal responsibility, in other-directedness.

If we are existing between these two realities, which we have designated by the terms Adamic Humanity and New Humanity, how do we move from the one to the other? What makes that movement possible? How do we become increasingly *free from* the one sphere and *free for* the other? The difference between participation in the one or the other is in *openness* and *empowerment*. In the *condition of separation*, our lives are *closed off* to the creative power of God, and therefore we are incapable of living within his purposes. But in the *restored relationship,* established by God's reconciling and forgiving act in Christ, we are *open to* the divine resources. Openness to the divine resources means that it is possible for God's love to flood our existence and to transform our relationships (5:5). Openness to the divine resources means that it is now possible for us to respond to the needs of *our world* on the basis of a joyful response to God's acceptance of us (5:1, 11; 15:7).

To be Christians means being called out of the inevitable and overwhelming bondage of the Adamic Humanity into the freedom and openness of the desert, where we stand between heaven and earth, between the call of the Eternal and the restraints of the temporal. It means that we have been to the mountaintop and have seen the Promised Land and therefore continue to live by the light of that vision. It means that we have received the gift of participation in a New Humanity and that this gift must be appropriated again and again.

The situation of the Christian may be presented in terms of two interlocking circles (see Diagram 2), where the new situation is represented by the area which is common to both circles. Participation in the nonshaded area of the Adamic Humanity is what Paul calls "bondage." Participation in the nonshaded area of the New Humanity would be a Christian version of Utopia, and the New Testament does not offer such a situation. Christians find themselves in the overlapping area of the two spheres of power. They are overshadowed by the one sphere, but also by the other. They are free for the one, but also for the other (illustrated by the horizontal arrows in the diagram). They are tempted by the allurements of the one and called by the radical but life-giving demands of the other.

A final illustration will hopefully drive home the point we have been trying to make and also provide a transition to the following chapter. Christian existence may be compared to a space capsule that is circling the earth. The capsule has been sprung loose from the gravitational pull of the earth by the thrust of a powerful Saturn rocket into a space where it is now potentially subject to the gravitational pull of celestial spheres other than the earth. Whether it ultimately returns to earth or succumbs to the gravitational force of another celestial sphere depends on the direction and timing of the thrust of its own small rockets. Christians have been torn loose from the gravitational bondage of the Adamic Humanity by the "power of God" and are now subject to the potential gravitational pull of the New Humanity. They exist in the space between the Earth and the Eternal, and movement toward the one or the other depends upon which way the power forces of freedom within are fired.

Questions for Reflection

1. Sin is the violation of other persons in human relationships. Discuss the often subtle ways in which such "sinning" manifests itself.
2. In what specific ways ought Christian responsibility to be worked out in overcoming the misuse of our natural environment?
3. Discuss various influences from society, culture, heritage, etc. which often shape our values, priorities, goals, life-styles, etc. Are Christians exempt from such influences? If not, how can we make sure that our lives are not shaped by them?
4. How do we discern between that which the lordship of Christ demands of us and the pressures that the culture brings to bear on us?
5. If increasing participation in the New Humanity depends upon an openness to the divine resources, how is such openness achieved?

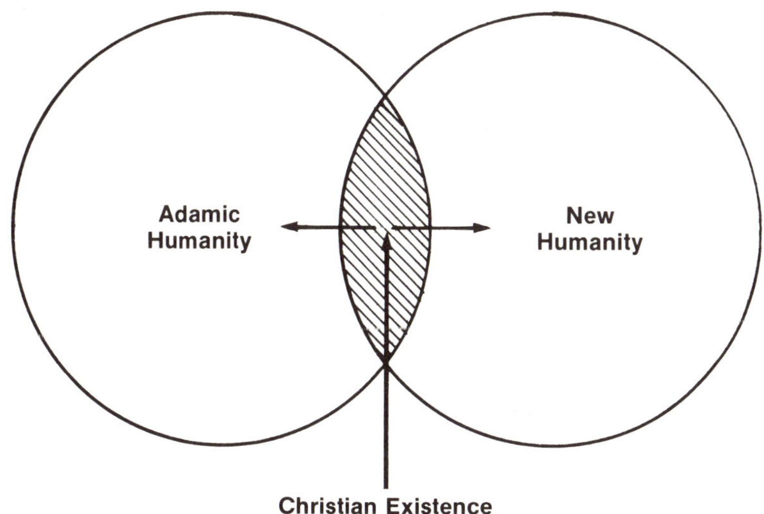

(Diagram 2)

CHAPTER 3

Between Death and Life

The theme of the entire chapter of Romans 6 points out the contrast between an existence which stands under the signature of death and an existence which stands under the signature of life. The former existence is in view when Christians permit their new situation to be infiltrated by the magnetic field of the Adamic Humanity. The latter is in view when Christians increasingly recognize and yield to the claims that the New Humanity has upon them.

The way of belonging to the New Humanity, established in Christ, is expressed by Paul in language which sounds, at best, strange to the modern ear and, at worst, incomprehensible.

He speaks, in the opening verses of chapter 6, about:

> being crucified with Christ;
> being buried with Christ;
> having died with Christ;
> being raised with Christ.

These phrases convey the idea of such an intense kind of union between the human being and the divine that we, who have been thoroughly conditioned by cold, rationalistic, scientific, technological, and computerized modes of thinking and existing, have immense difficulty in grasping the meaning of such concepts.[1] Even the way in which we express our piety and our forms of worship have been affected by this twentieth-century mentality. A friend recently shared with me his impressions of a series of worship services, which he had attended, of a quite average and representative Protestant congregation. He compared his experience to the experience which he has daily in his job at the factory: the processes are computerized, the conveyor belts deliver specified products to specified destinations at specified times. The personnel at the assembly lines perform their assigned duties. And the bell at 4 P.M. brings the experience to a predetermined conclusion. My friend's criticism was that there was no time for meditation, for reflection, for getting in touch with his feelings. I have a suspicion that at least one of the reasons for the flight of so many of our young people into Eastern mysticism and the occult, with their meditation and inwardness, is the failure of our civilized, acculturated form of Christianity to provide them with a sense of the mysterious, of the "otherness" of the divine. We have so often and so largely domesticated the divine that our youth, instinctively sensing the wrongness of it, have fled from this counterfeit image. We have often heard, in many quarters, that the gospel is "simple," that all that is necessary for the attainment of LIFE is simple faith. If that means that the response of faith to God is like the genuine trusting response of the child to the love of a parent, then I agree. But it seems that too often the assertion of the "simplicity" of the gospel and faith has served to rob the whole matter of the dimension of the eternal, has emptied it of its awesome dimensions. We must begin to recover, for our time, a sense of the mystery of life and a sense of the limited nature of our own perception and ability to comprehend that mystery.

Paul's idea of *being in Christ,* or *being united with Christ,* has frequently been referred to as "Pauline mysticism," where "mysticism" designates a particularly intense correspondence between the human being and the divine. What did Paul really mean when he used such mystical language? Can we really grasp what Paul felt and intended to communicate when he said, "I have been crucified with Christ; it is no longer I who live, but Christ who lives in me . . ." (Galatians 2:20)? What was Paul's understanding of the nature of the mystical relationship between the believer and his Lord?

Some years ago, the German scholar Adolf Deissmann made the attempt to answer that question by comparing Paul's statements with the other religions and philosophies of the ancient Near East. He found that at many points there was a vast difference between the way many of these understood our relationship with God and how that relationship was expressed by Paul. The boiled-down presentation of the contrasts worked out by Deissmann[2] (see

Diagram 3) should help us to a better perception of that which, for Paul, is essential in the divine-human relationships.

TWO WAYS IN WHICH "RELIGION" MANIFESTS ITSELF

OR

1. humankind approaches God	God approaches humankind
performance	grace
striving	divine gift
2. asserts humankind's ability to control and manipulate God	affirms willingness to be controlled by God
3. results in a loss of human personality; denies personality	results in the sanctification of the personality through the presence of God; affirms personality
4. egocentric religion	theocentric religion
5. characterized by enthusiastic intoxication	characterized by ethical enthusiasm

(Diagram 3)

Even a cursory scanning of the contrasts between the left- and right-hand sides of the list will convince us that Paul's understanding of the divine-human relationship must be located on the right-hand side of the contrast. Let us briefly comment upon the various components of that list.

1. A reading of Paul's letters will convince us that, for him, true religion does not originate with us, but rather with God. We do not, by our demonstrations of piety and devotion, establish human-divine interaction. It is God who has taken the initiative, who has broken into a "world in revolt" and calls us to find ourselves and our fellows in the context of a restored relationship with himself. Grace is the hallmark of that action, and the resulting relationship is a divine gift.

2. In that relationship, we are in no position to control God. Religion becomes bankrupt at precisely that point where its practitioners fall prey to the illusion that religious acts or words have power over God. Paganism is shot through and through with such a magical conception of religious formulations and religious

acts. And there was much of such paganism in the religious attitude and practice of Jesus' and Paul's co-religionists. Jesus criticized the kind of praying which consists of the "heaping up of empty phrases" as something which the Gentiles did: ". . . they think that they will be heard for their many words" (Matthew 6:7). Again, the story about the itinerant Jewish exorcists in Acts 19:13-19, who sought to cast out evil spirits by "pronouncing the name of the Lord Jesus," is a clear illustration of the religious mentality which asserts ability to control God or to be in control of divine power. For Paul, God is in control, and whatever manifestation of divine power there is, it is not at the disposal of the human vessel, but remains at the disposal of the Potter who made the vessel.

3. In the relationship thus instituted by God, there can be, for Paul, no overpowering or elimination of the human personality by the divine, as was the case in many other religions at the time of early Christianity. In Christianity, the purpose of religion is *not* the deification of persons, *but* the humanizing of persons; *not* their increasingly closer approximation to the divine, *but* their closer approximation to that which is most fully human; *not* the denial of the human personality, *but* the affirmation of the human personality; *not* the elimination of an individual's particular personality traits, *but* the sanctification of those personality traits. The matter may be stated in no uncertain terms: to the extent that religious affirmation and practice violates our personalities and calls us into conformity with a faceless "Christian ideal personality," religion ceases to be Christian. The purpose of redemption is the transformation of the human person toward its intended wholeness, not its metamorphosis into something else!

4. The divine-human relationship, expressed in those mystical terms of intimacy by Paul, is most centrally characterized by theocentricity and the rejection of egocentricity. That is to say, we do not enter into and affirm and nurture the relationship for our own benefit, for personal "rewards" and "blessings," but rather out of a free and joyful response of gratefulness to the One who has broken into the chaos of our lives and has reclaimed us as his children. The religions within the environment of early Christianity were filled with those trappings which revealed that their major purpose was procuring all sorts of benefits for the worshiper. Religion was a means toward specific egocentric ends: procuring the favor of the god(s), health, good and plentiful crops, protection from potential enemies, immortality, etc. Even ancient Hebrew religious thought contained some of these egocentric

elements. In popularized form, the central religious formulation went something like this: *If* you wish to obtain the blessings of earthly goods, health, long life, and children, *then* keep the statutes of the Lord your God. The Book of Job is a devastating polemic against that view of the nature and purpose of religion. Job's friends clung to the pagan notion that there is a one-to-one correspondence between God's favor and earthly blessings and between God's anger and human calamity. But Job, who had been robbed of all those external signs which *supposedly* indicate the soundness of a person's relation with the Divine, clung to the faith that his relationship with God was unmarred and hoped for final vindication. In his own cynical way, the author of Ecclesiastes looks at the reality of life about him and comes to the conclusion that there simply is no direct correspondence between true religious faith and earthly blessings. In fact, he affirms that often those most intimately related to God suffer the most on this earth. The existence of martyrs throughout the ages, who have suffered persecution and died for their faith, certainly underlines his observation. Paul, too, before Damascus, was caught up in a kind of "tit-for-tat" religiosity. He participated in a legalistic tradition which held that God's relationship with Israel and his saving action toward it were contingent upon the quantity of righteous deeds done in Israel. But his experience of being grasped by Christ (see Philippians 3:12) convinced him that that kind of religion had upon it the stench of death. Religion, according to Paul, is not a means to an end; it is an end in itself. The purpose of the creature's relationship with the Creator is not the achievement of some other goal; rather, the purpose of the creature's relationship with the Creator *is that relationship.* The old Westminster Confession put it well when it said that "the purpose of man is to glorify God and to enjoy him forever." And "to glorify God" does not mean to sit around and sing praises, but to live out of the relationship with God in such a way that God's purposes for human existence are realized.

5. Finally, Paul's mysticism, his view of the relationship between the believer and Christ, is characterized by *ethical enthusiasm.* Paul recognized that the divine-human relationship had to work itself out in the arena of human relationships. At that point his ideas differed markedly from those of many other religions practiced in his environment. Especially in the mystery cults which flourished at that time, there was almost a complete break between cult and ethics. The devotees of these mystery religions participated in the religious ceremonies, underwent

rituals of purification, were caught up in phenomenal spiritual experiences, and often became involved in ecstatic utterances. But their religions made no ethical demands, called for no transformation of life-style, did not insist on moral behavior. Apparently, there were converts from these mystery religions in the Pauline congregations who had imported some elements from their former cults into their Christian existence. Paul's devastating attack on the spiritual enthusiasts at Corinth is a case in point, and chapter 13 of First Corinthians is the clarion trumpet blast against all forms of enthusiastic intoxication, as well as the loftiest call for ethical enthusiasm ever uttered. Spiritual experiences, no matter how lofty, must be judged as ultimately empty if they do not usher us out into the world of action.

The reason why we have had so much difficulty understanding Paul's "mysticism," and attempting to live out of it, is at least in part that we have often "paganized" that mysticism, that we have actually practiced our faith as if it were characterized by the items on the left-hand side of the list (in Diagram 3).

1. We seek to secure our position before God and to gain his approval of us by the performance of "religious duties": attendance at religious functions, going through particular religious exercises, participating in "the work of the church." We equate the American ideal of "success" with God's will, and so we play the "numbers game": "God must certainly be pleased with our efforts to have the largest church school attendance in our district (even if our methods for procuring that large attendance may be somewhat questionable!). And he certainly will applaud the fact that our mission budget exceeds that of every other church in the convention (even though the bulk of it comes from several wealthy contributors!). And oh, how glad he must be that we have more activities going on in our church building than most other churches in this town (even though all that activity is simply adding another nail to the coffin of the disintegration of our families!)." We do not really understand what it means to be "crucified with Christ" and to live out of that reality, because we have slipped a paganistic religion of performance in through the back door of our Christian existence, and the infiltration is producing a counterfeit form of Christianity.

2. Is not much of our "Christian practice" also characterized by the subtle assumption that we possess the ability to control God? Much of our understanding and use of prayer is a case in point. It is actually amazing how frequently we use prayer as a means of

twisting the arm of God toward a particular end, or as a trump card. We pray for good weather for the church school picnic, with the expectation that if our prayers are fervent and intense and sincere enough, God will do as we wish. We pray for the restoration of health, with the assumption that if health does not come, the prayer has not been fervent enough or for some reason has been ineffective. We have the idea that if enough of us get together to pray, the cumulative weight of the words spoken will move God to act in accordance with our purposes. All of these concepts, and the more subtle variations thereof, are pagan, not Christian! A friend once told me that prayer was blasphemy. From his perspective as an atheist he was right; but at the same time he revealed a true understanding of the nature and purpose of prayer. Prayer, he said, is blasphemy against persons, because prayer is an indication of human weakness. Prayer, in the Christian scheme, submits us to the control of God. It is that human act which places us at the disposal of the Creator; it does not place the Creator at our disposal. Prayer is that human act which aligns us with God's purposes; it does not align him with our purposes!

We have understood and used "faith" in a very similar vein. We have talked of "faith" as if it were a quantitative "thing" of which we could have more or less. From such a conception of "faith," stepping into the belief that the exercise of "sufficient faith" will move the Divine into action has been easy. The experience of a pastor brought the tragedy of such a view of faith into bold relief for me. In his youth he had been robbed of 90 percent of his sight by a disease. In faith before his Maker he had accepted that condition and had courageously and joyfully lived out of it in fruitful and helpful presence among others. But in recent association with a community of Christians, he has increasingly been confronted with the suggestion that, if he had only *more faith*, God would heal him. The experience has virtually shattered him. Faith, like love, is not something that can be measured. (My wife would be horrified to learn that my love for her was parceled out in two- or five- or ten-pound packages, depending on how I felt about her at any one time!) When Jesus speaks of faith in terms of little children or tiny mustard seeds, he is not speaking about "amounts" of faith, but about a "quality of life." Faith is the response of trust, of allegiance, of commitment to God, not a magical substance which induces God to jump when we tell him to. We have misunderstood what it means to be "buried with Christ" when we practice a form of religion which asserts our ability to control God.

3. The denial of personality, which had such a prominent place in the pagan mystery cults and in some forms of Christian mysticism in the Middle Ages, also raises its head again and again and thus stretches the tentacles of paganism into Christian practice. No one has succeeded better in focusing on that problem than C. S. Lewis in *The Screwtape Letters.* In a correspondence from Screwtape to Wormwood, one of his devilish lieutenants who is assigned to deal with a recent human convert to Christianity, the following instruction is given:

> Keep his mind on the inner life. He thinks his conversion is something *inside* him. . . . Keep his mind off the most elementary duties by directing it to the most advanced and spiritual ones.
> . . . Make sure that [his prayers] are always . . . concerned with the state of [his mother's] soul and never with her rheumatism. . . . I have had patients of my own so well in hand that they could be turned at a moment's notice from impassioned prayer for a wife's or son's "soul" to beating or insulting the real wife or son without a qualm.[3]

The point made by Lewis needs little comment. It is an illustration of depersonalization by seeing the other as nothing but a "soul" to be saved, to be cleansed and fitted for its eternal destiny. In my student days a fellow seminarian once told me that being there for persons in need was, for him, always a means for witness and a call for the other person to "be saved." He virtually seized upon "need situations" as opportunities for confrontation. In that kind of "evangelistic scheme," persons become objects: persons in need are not helped because they are in need, but because they are a "case"; they are not helped because they are human persons whose burdens we are constrained to carry by the love of Christ, but because they are potential "stars in our crown."

4. We have difficulty in comprehending what it means to "live with Christ" because much of the manifestation of our Christian existence is characterized by egocentricity. We are all familiar with a method of evangelism which emphasizes "fear tactics" as a means of ushering persons through the eternal portals into the kingdom of God. That is a method which plays upon egocentric motivations. I recently read the sermon of a pastor who boasts one of the largest church schools in the nation. The central theme of the forty-minute harangue was this: "Respond to God before your child is struck down in an accident; give your life to Christian ministry before God punishes you with cancer of the throat; heed God's demand for your tithe before he causes your business to

crumble; say yes to God before he afflicts your wife with a terminal disease."

That is surely the grossest perversion of the biblical understanding of God and of his intent for the nature of our response to him. But this "tit-for-tat" kind of religiosity often raises its head in much subtler ways which get much closer to where many of us are living our lives. Thus, the paganistic hangover represented in the attitude of Job's friends is still very widespread. We look upon our earthly possessions and say rather piously, "The Lord has been good to me," which, in translation, often means, "I have lived righteously, therefore I have been blessed by God." Or, we survey our health, attribute it to "right living," and credit God with the good sense of having seen our "righteousness" and, in reward for it, keeping dangerous bacteria away from us. The implication of such an attitude is of course that there is something amiss in the religion of those who do not have equivalent possessions or good health.

There is, further, the common perception of Christian existence in capitalistic terms: the more we invest, the more we get out. We really cater to those of means in the congregation, with the explicit or implicit suggestion that God is surely going to prosper the giver in direct proportion to the size of the gift. The donation of time and brains and muscle is also frequently drawn into this investment scheme: if we only become involved enough, give enough time, do enough, then God will surely come across with substantial dividends. That is egocentric religion, and it is a pagan perversion of Christian faith!

5. Finally, there is that form of Christianity which majors in "spiritual experiences" but minors in "practical acts." It is a form which is attractive for many, especially for those who have experienced "religion without emotion"; but it must be judged as inadequate on the basis of Paul's understanding of the divine-human relationship.

There is, in our day, a revival of enthusiasm which has blown fresh life into dry and dead religious bones in many quarters. But there are extreme manifestations of the charismatic renewal which must be rejected as decidedly unbiblical. Enthusiastic spiritual intoxication, with the corresponding phenomena of extraordinary powers and ecstatic utterances, *may be* valid experiences, but they are *not necessarily* so, and the attempt to universalize those experiences and make them the normative criteria for true spirituality simply misses the whole thrust of the New Testament. There, the normative criterion for true spirituality is ethical action:

being an edifying, healing, loving, forgiving, helping presence in the midst of God's world. Enthusiastic intoxication, without ethical enthusiasm, is empty.

Again, in many sectors of the Christian church, the small-group movement has brought new vitality and wholeness into the lives of countless Christians who were previously caught up in a more or less perfunctory religiosity. But here, as in other countertrends, the swing of the pendulum has at times gone to the other extreme. In the context of intense personal relationships within small groups, feelings, experiences, emotions have at times been emphasized to such an extent that other aspects of personhood, such as rationality and volition, have been neglected. A phrase from a popular gospel song illustrates this kind of emphasis:

> You ask me how I know He lives,
> He lives within my heart.

I have had students who were convinced that their feelings provided the final index for truth. A focusing on feelings—which can be deceptive—can easily degenerate into what might be called a "touchy-feely" sort of interaction between persons. It is the experience for the sake of the experience: "I feel, I feel, I know not what I feel, but let me feel it again." Experiential enthusiasm is no substitute for ethical enthusiasm. Ethics without enthusiasm can easily lead to a cold moral legalism. Experiential enthusiasm, without ethics, is finally inadequate.

In the foregoing discussion, the attempt was made to look at Paul's mysticism—his understanding of those elements that characterize the divine-human relationship—in overall terms. Let us now take a closer look at Paul's precise language in Romans 6:1-10.

For the purpose of gaining a total perspective, the significant phrases from the passage are grouped together under three general headings (see Diagram 4). The way of entering the New Humanity is by *means* of an intense union with Christ which Paul communicates by use of the baptismal imagery. The way of belonging to the New Humanity is indicated by a statement of both *positive* and *negative results*.

Now what is extremely interesting, as well as puzzling, about these statements by Paul is that we have, side by side, *statements of fact* and *statements of possibility*. In Greek, the indicative mood is employed to make factual assertions. In our passage, Paul uses it to assert that Christians *are* dead to sin, free from sin, crucified with Christ, etc. That is, he expresses the "is-ness," the givenness, of a particular condition. Again, in Greek, the subjunctive mood is employed to indicate possibility. Paul uses it in those phrases which are in bold face in the diagram. What we have, therefore, is an internal tension between the affirmation that we died to sin, and are therefore free from its bondage, and the assertion that such freedom is always and only present as a possibility *which can find actualization.* Let us take a look at the nature of that *indicative,* that *is-ness,* and then inquire as to the relation between it and the affirmation of it as possibility.

How is that is-ness of the Christian's mystical relationship with Christ to be understood? In the attempt to answer that question, we are confronted with the baptismal language (6:3-4). Paul clearly associates the baptism event with the death and resurrection of Christ and with our dying to sin and rising to newness of life. What is the meaning of that association? This is not the place to enter into a discussion on the multifaceted matter of Christian baptism, except briefly to indicate the main answers that have been given to the above question and to explore another perspective.

(Diagram 4)

MEANS

6:3 baptized into Christ
baptized into his death

6:4 buried with him by baptism into death

6:5 united with him in a death like his

6:8 we have died with Christ

RESULT (negative)

6:2 we died to sin

6:6 Our old self was crucified with him that our sin-dominated existence **might be abolished** that we **might no longer be enslaved** by sin

6:7 he who has died is freed from sin

RESULT (positive)

6:4 as Christ was raised from the dead so we **might walk** in newness of life

6:5 we shall be united with him in a resurrection like his

6:8 we shall live with him

In the early centuries of the Christian era, the church increasingly interpreted the baptism event in *sacramental-magical* terms. It was believed that something actually happened in the event; that the act itself mediated to the person undergoing baptism the saving qualities of the death and resurrection of Christ. Thus, infant baptism was seen as an effective event, even though no faith on the infant's part was present.

The various reformation movements, from the fifteenth century on, more or less rejected such a sacramental understanding in favor of what may be designated a *mystical-spiritual* interpretation. Here, the baptismal event signaled the real presence of the crucified and risen Christ and an inward, spiritual union between Christ and the one being baptized.

In rejecting infant baptism as not valid, the Baptist tradition, along with other sectarian movements, also rejected the interpretation of the meaning and nature of the event associated largely with infant baptism. It was argued that the act of baptism, in and of itself, accomplishes nothing; that it is in the context of personal decision, commitment, and faith where one enters into relationship with Christ. The baptismal event *merely symbolizes* that prior commitment.

That baptism, especially by immersion, symbolizes death and resurrection is beyond question. But in our reaction against any form of sacramentalism, we have often in practice swung to the other extreme. By emphasizing that the act is *merely* symbolic, it has been emptied of any real significance, beyond the perfunctory necessary requirement for entrance into most of our Baptist churches. The logical and inevitable consequence of such a devaluation of the event has been a Baptist version of infant baptism with semi-sacramental characteristics. By the time our children reach the Middler or Junior Departments of our church school programs, every effort has been made to get them to make a personal decision of faith; then we quickly seal that decision by baptizing them and entering their names on the church's rolls. (Such figures look good in the statistics published by the church!) The majority of students whom I have asked concerning their baptism have indicated that the event was largely a perfunctory exercise.

Let us take another look at that strange, mystical language with which Paul describes our entrance into the New Humanity. If we look at baptism against the background of the *relationship* categories worked out in the previous chapters, then it may be possible to understand it not in *sacramental* or *spiritual* or *symbolic* terms, but in *relational terms.* In the event of baptism, we affirm that our lives are henceforth *to be determined* by the fact that Christ has died and was raised, that *in relationship with him* we are *delivered* from death's dominion and *freed for life.* If the "with Christ" or "in Christ" language expresses a *relational reality,* then it is possible to understand the close connection between baptism and the forgiveness of sins (see Acts 2:38). By being baptized, believers affirm that:

—in their relation with Christ, their sins find forgiveness
—in their relation with Christ, new life is created within them
—in their relation with Christ, they are in touch with the continuing source of their own lives
—in their relation with Christ, they find continuing renewal and regeneration
—in their relation with Christ, the burdens of life become bearable
—in their relation with Christ, the hang-ups and habits and bondages of life can be overcome.

Such a relational understanding of baptism, as well as of the new existence which it initiates, makes it possible to come to grips with the paradoxical contradiction between two statements by Paul in chapter 6:

6:7—He who has died is freed from sin.
6:12—Let not sin therefore reign in your mortal bodies. . . .

New life, says Paul, has become both *a reality* and *a possibility.* How do we know that? Paul's answer is given in 6:9-10—Christ is alive; death no longer has dominion over him. Therefore, according to verse 6:11, we can *affirm* that in relationship with Christ we are *free from sin* and *alive to God.* Verse 6:11 is the climactic *affirmation of the reality of a relationship.* Verses 6:12-23 outline the *practical outworking of this reality* (see Diagram 5).

This juxtaposition may best be illustrated by an analysis of intense human relationships in which commitment and love are central factors. The clearest example is the marriage relationship. It exists on two levels:

1. *Relational reality,* consisting of mutual commitment in love and interdependence.
2. *Practical incarnation of that reality,* of that commitment, in concrete acts, in concrete existence.

It is clear that number 2 does not flow automatically or inevitably out of number 1, as C. S. Lewis has said by means of the intercepted correspondence between Screwtape and Wormwood:

> . . . [There is the possibility of] disappointment . . . on the threshold of every human endeavour. . . . It occurs when lovers have got married and begin the real task of learning to live together. . . . [There is] the transition from dreaming aspiration to laborious doing.[4]

There must constantly be movement from *affirmation* to *incarnation,* or else the relationship is in difficulty. There is constantly the temptation—whether consciously recognized or not—"to look at another woman with lust," to separate ourselves from the loved one, to use and misuse the other, to ignore the other, to "do our own thing" without regard for the other, to hide our real self from the other. These threats to the relationship must be rejected again and again as we reaffirm our love and commitment and interdependence. To be married means that our lives are governed by the continual *affirmation* and *incarnation* of the commitments in that relationship. To be "in Christ"—to be united with him in death and resurrection—means that our lives are governed by the continual *affirmation* and *incarnation* of the commitments in that relationship. Not to be so determined is to have an existence which Paul describes as "death." To be so determined is to have an existence which Paul describes as "life." Because our relationship with Christ must be reaffirmed and reincarnated in our daily existence, we stand again and again at the threshold of decision between death and life.

What does our existence look like when this affirmation and incarnation are missing? When our relationship with Christ does not impinge upon the concrete living which we do, then *other relationships* will certainly fill this vacuum. If it is not *that Lord* whose mind is being brought to bear upon our human relationships, then *other lords* will most certainly bring their minds to bear upon those relationships.

Parents are models for their children, whether they like it or not. Our children sense very quickly who we are and what the lords and gods are at whose altars we serve. So the questions for me as a father are these: Does my young son sense, as he is maturing, that my life is ruled by a higher kind of authority than tomorrow's paycheck, the expectations of my neighbors, the priority of *things* over persons? Does he sense, as he observes my relationship with his mother, that we share a *real* love, that we are truly there for one another, that we keep pace, in that relationship, to a "different drummer"? To the extent that he senses these things, my existence is an incarnation of my relationship with Christ; my existence is lived under the shadow of the word "life." To the extent that he does not observe these, my existence is the incarnation of *other* relationships; it is lived under the shadow of the shrines of *other* gods and stands therefore under the signature of "death."

Christian existence is an existence between the polarities of life and death. The questions are: Which of these has for us the stronger magnetic force? Which of these two magnetic fields is increasingly claiming our attention? Which of these two poles increasingly determines the priorities by which we order our lives?

Questions for Reflection

1. What does your baptism mean to you? What ought it to mean in terms of your ongoing life?
2. Think about the various characteristics that distinguish Christian faith—as rooted in the New Testament—from a counterfeit form; then discuss ways in which counterfeit elements manifest themselves in our "religious activity."
3. What would the presence of *ethical enthusiasm* look like in our individual and congregational life?
4. Much of our religious practice evidences an understanding of religion as a *means toward an end*. What is problematic about that?
5. What is your understanding of prayer? How is it related to God's purposes for us?

6:1-11

the INDICATIVE

(**is**-ness)—**affirmation of the reality of a relationship**

6:12-19

the IMPERATIVE

(**ought**-ness)—**practical outworking of that relationship**

(Diagram 5)

CHAPTER 4

Between Religion Which Enslaves and Religion Which Frees

We have been called out of the bondage of the Adamic Humanity into a New Humanity which is characterized by freedom before God and genuine life with our fellow human beings. In that sense, Christian faith is a freeing experience. But when the shadow of the Adamic Humanity is permitted to impinge upon that new existence, when the magnetic force of "existence unto death" claims our allegiance, then the result is often a religious experience or life-style which enslaves rather than frees. It is this possibility of an enslaving religious experience to which Paul turns in chapter 7 of Romans. Let us then follow him into this territory of the tension between "religious captivity" and "religious freedom."

A key text in Romans 7 is verse 15: "I do not understand my own actions. For I *do not* do what I want, but I *do* the very thing I hate" (italics added). On plain reading, what we have here is the candid confession of a basic split in human personality, of neurotic impotence, of utter weakness. Paul's final analysis of it is caught up in the word "wretchedness" (see 7:24).

If Romans 7:7-24 is a description of what Christian existence is all about, then it stands in stark contrast to the kind of joy and freedom and newness with which Paul characterized Christian existence in chapters 5-6. If chapter 7 is a statement about the final situation of the Christian, then I find it unattractive. If the invitation of God does not lead to a new kind of life, it is not "good news" at all, but really "bad news."

And yet, the common and prevailing interpretation of Romans

holds that Paul is speaking about an *internal tension* between the Christian's *higher* and *lower* self. Such an understanding of Christian life and faith is based on two mistaken premises.

The first is the idea that the *justification event* creates a new moral-ethical core which then has to fight it out with the rest of our beings—primarily our "baser instincts," our "flesh" with its passions and desires.

We have attempted to show, in chapter 2 above, that such an understanding of the salvation event simply does not do justice to the New Testament's understanding of the salvation of the *whole person.* For if *we* cannot do what we want and instead do the very thing we hate, then, in Paul's terms, we are enslaved and have not really experienced the reconciling and freeing dimensions of God's saving love through Christ.

The second mistaken premise consists of a misinterpretation of the passage before us. This misinterpretation is the result of two factors:

1. a misreading of *Paul's terminology;*
2. a misreading of the *structure of the text* and thus of the intention of the author.

Let us examine these two aspects in turn.

1. *Terminology:* The troublesome word in the text of Romans 7:5-25 is the word *flesh.* It is used several times in this text (vv. 5, 18, 25) in close association throughout with *sin* and *death* and their dominion. The use of the word "flesh" with these negative associations, in opposition to the "I" which has higher aspirations, is largely responsible for the view that Romans 7 insists upon a *divided self,* in which unceasing warfare is raging.

In chapter 3 of this book, we maintained that when Paul speaks about being "in the flesh" he does not speak about *physicalness* as such, about physical passions and appetites, but rather about a *way of life,* an *orientation of life,* a *life lived outside the purposes of God for us.* Such an understanding of Paul's use of the term "flesh" is clearly present in a number of passages both outside and within Romans 7. The Ephesians are told (Ephesians 2:1-3) that they have been made alive, that they have been grasped out of a condition characterized by "the passions of our flesh." The passage then goes on to explain in more detail what "passions of our flesh" means: namely, "desires of body and mind." This shows that for Paul the term "flesh"—in its *religious* usage—is not so much a biological term. It is a comprehensive term, including what to the Greek audience was the highest part of the human person, the mind. A similar use of the term "flesh" appears in Romans 8, where Paul is drawing a contrast between two ways of existing and characterizes one way with the phrases:

> —living according to the flesh
> —setting the mind on the flesh
> —being in the flesh.

Then he goes on to say: "But you are not in the flesh." It is obvious that the word "flesh" is not employed here in any biological sense! The *religious* use of the word "flesh" makes it possible for Paul to say that there was a time when we were living in the flesh (Romans 7:5)—though he obviously recognizes that Christians continue to be physical creatures.

When Paul therefore contrasts a "fleshly" way of existing with a "spiritual" way of existing, he is *not* speaking about two distinct parts of the person, *but* about two possible orientations of the person.

The reason why the word "flesh" is used to denote an existence out of tune with God is that it is ultimately in the arena of the physical that the unrelatedness between man and God most specifically manifests itself.[1] But we remember that Jesus, before Paul, had already pointed out that the origin of murder or adultery is *at the core of man's being.*

Therefore, the contrast which Paul makes between the "I" on the one hand and "my flesh" on the other (7:18) is not a contrast between a higher and lower self. Rather, the "I" is the *total self* insofar as it affirms the good or the will of God as expressed in the law. "My flesh" is the *total self* insofar as it is powerless, insofar as it is dominated by sin, insofar as it is unrelated to God.

With this overall perspective in mind, let us now turn to the structure of the argument, to see what it is that Paul is getting at here.

2. *Structure of the text:* I want to begin with a basic thesis, and then work through the text to illustrate that thesis. *Romans 7:7-25 is not a description of Christian existence, of life in Christ.* For everything which Paul says about Christian existence throughout his letters stands diametrically opposed to the kind of existence which he describes in 7:7-25. For purposes of clarity, it may be helpful to make a list of the statements which Paul uses in 7:7-25 to describe a certain kind of existence and to place it side by side with a list of statements which specifically describe "life in Christ." The two lists are presented under two headings which emerge out of the verses 7:5 and 7:6.

Then (7:5)	**Now (7:6)**
Existence unto Death	**Existence unto Life**
7:7-25	8:1-39
—sinful passions aroused by law	—discharged from the law
—fruit for death	—no longer captive under it
—covetousness	—new life of the Spirit
—"death" in the midst of continued physical life	—freed from death-dominated existence
—sold under sin	—alive toward God
—dominated by sin	—led by the Spirit children of God
—captive to law of sin	—glorious liberty
—death-dominated existence	—empowerment in weakness
—wretchedness and despair	—no outside power can separate us from God's love

The preceding presentation is intended to illustrate graphically the structure of Paul's argument. It becomes clear that verses 5 and 6 are the headlines for what follows through the end of chapter 8:

Verse 5 is explicated in the rest of chapter 7.

Verse 6 is explicated in chapter 8.

But if, as I have maintained, chapter 7 is not a description of genuine Christian existence, what is it? What kind of existence does it describe and analyze?

Chapter 7:7-25 provides an *autobiographical flashback*—from the viewpoint of Paul's Christian experience—of life under the law, *life lived by means of external conformity to a code of conduct.* Because it presents an autobiographical flashback, it is therefore told partially in the *first person singular* and in the *present tense* (especially in vv. 14-25).

As a Jew, Paul never could have said what he says here about the connection between law and sin. That would have been preposterous! For the giving of the law to Israel was understood in Judaism as a *gift of God,* as a sign of his grace and favor. Indeed, the law was seen as that which made life in community possible.[2] However, from the point of view of his Christian experience, Paul realized that the life which he had lived in strictest conformity to that standard had in it ultimately the seeds of death. The well-known passage in Philippians 3:4-8, where Paul describes his blamelessness under the law as finally worthless, shows that his Christian experience gave him a new perspective on a law-oriented religious life-style.

Let us now trace the movement of Paul's argument in verses 7-25. For clarification, the argument will be summarized.

> 7:5 In light of the fact that the *law* is *that reality* which exposes human life for what it really is, namely *life characterized by sin and death,*
>
> 7:7 is the law then sin?
>
> 7:7-14*a* The answer of this entire passage is "No!" because the law is holy and spiritual;
>
> > the commandment is holy, just, and good.
>
> *Hypothetical Question:*
> Why then is man in this predicament?
>
> 7:14*b* *Gives the Answer:*
> "I am carnal" (Let us remember at this point our discussion above on the meaning of Paul's use of the term "flesh": fleshly existence
>
> > —is existence dominated by sin.
> > —is life apart from dependence on God's grace.)
>
> 7:15-24 *Explains the Answer* given in 14*b*.
>
> 7:15-16 *Statement of the Argument:*
> In that kind of existence (fleshly), *despair of failure* is the characteristic trademark:
>
> > —even when the recognition of the goodness of the law is present.
> > —even when the intention to live in keeping with that goodness is present.
>
> Nonetheless, "concrete existence" does not correspond to that high intention and recognition.
>
> 7:17-23 *Summary of the Argument:*
> So I am really powerless: goodness does not finally characterize a life lived apart from dependence upon God's grace. The human being, *even the religious one,* is a slave. As such, he or she cannot bring his or her life into conformity with God's intention.
>
> 7:24 *Conclusion:*
> Wretched person that I am, who will deliver me from this death-dominated existence?

7:25 *Resolution:*

> Thanks be to God! Through Jesus Christ I can be set free from this desperate condition in which, though I acknowledge the goodness of God's law, my concrete existence does violence to that understanding.

What Paul has given us in these verses of chapter 7 is a description of the *ultimate futility* of a life lived in external conformity to a set of injunctions and prohibitions, even if these injunctions and prohibitions do come out of the very Word of God!

What then is the relevance for Christian existence of this description? It lies in the recognition that *where the real thing is present, the counterfeit is never far behind.* Paul's entire missionary activity was again and again overshadowed by a *counterfeit form of Christian existence,* and he waged a life and death struggle against it. His writings are punctuated by polemical crescendos against a form of Christian existence in which external conformity to legal requirements leads to enslavement, to bondage, to despair. A brief selection of passages from Paul's letters underlines his concern that Christian faith be not usurped and overwhelmed by a counterfeit form:

Romans 8:15	. . . you did not receive the spirit of slavery. . . .
Galatians 3:1-3	O foolish Galatians! Who has bewitched you? . . . Having begun with the Spirit, are you now ending with the flesh [legal requirement]?
Galatians 4:9-10	. . . How can you turn back again to the weak and beggarly elemental spirits, whose slaves you want to be once more? You observe days, and months, and seasons, and years!
Galatians 5:1	For freedom Christ has set us free; . . . do not submit again to a yoke of slavery.
Colossians 2:20-23	Why do you submit to [rules and] regulations, "Do not handle, Do not taste, Do not touch." . . . These have indeed an appearance of . . . [rigorous] devotion . . . but they are of no value. . . .

It is clear from these powerful statements that Paul wanted to save his Christian congregations from a form of religious piety and practice which was ultimately empty and lifeless. Now there is a form of Christian existence in our own time which fits the Pauline polemic quite well; and *by Paul's standards, it is counterfeit*

Christianity. It is an existence characterized by the following:

1. *Rules and regulations.* "Do not handle, Do not taste, Do not touch." Here "true spirituality" is measured by the degree to which a person can keep him or herself undefiled from any number of "worldly" things. The various lists of prohibitions clearly define what is worldly and therefore off limits. What we have in all of this is a "Christian" counterpart to the Pharisaic demands for external purity. We are well aware of Jesus' attitude toward that kind of religious mentality!

2. *Clearly defined codes of behavior.* "Do not go to . . ." or "Do not associate with . . ." or "Do not participate in. . . ." I recently heard the pastor of a large congregation pronounce that he had a direct word of God for them and then proceeded to lay down that direct commandment: "Do not go to see the film 'The Exorcist,' because you will be defiled by this film which was conceived in the bowels of hell!" As pastoral advice and counsel, such a statement may have been good and proper. But attaching to it divine sanction and laying it down as religious law to confine and define the behavior of Christians is quite another matter. It presumes the ability to determine the limits of Christian behavior and leads inevitably—as it did in Pharisaic Judaism—to a religion of law in which the traditions of humans occupy the throne.

3. *Particular external manifestations of piety* from which there can be no departure. Here, adherence to a calendar of religious activities—such as attendance at a specific number of services or meetings in the church—is normative for the measure of a person's "orthodoxy." When a congregation does not have a particular kind of Sunday evening service, it is judged as not "being alive spiritually" or as "going liberal." Again, the measure of devotion and the depth of orthodoxy are evaluated by conformity to externals such as the mode of dress or the length of skirt or hair. An extreme example from a letter to the editor of a religious periodical is here given:

> I don't agree . . . that it doesn't matter how long hair is or how we dress. God's Word says, "Be not conformed to this world. . . ." So if we dress like the world, how do we prove that our mind has been renewed? His Word also tells women to dress decently. Well, I would hardly call a wife or a mother in pants suits dressed decently. . . .
> Do these women honestly believe God approves of them looking like boys, with their hair cut so short?[3]

It would be easy to dismiss such an extreme view of "religion by externals," but we are doubtless well aware of subtler forms of judging the level of people's Christian commitments on the basis of externals. One such external manifestation of piety is tied to a particular kind of vocabulary. The person who does not express his or her faith in "traditional" terms and phrases becomes immediately suspect. The pastor who speaks about "becoming whole" is criticized for not emphasizing the necessity of "being born again." On the other hand, the person whose "religious language" or prayer is studded with divine names and sacred formulas, such as "the atoning blood of Jesus," has passed the test of orthodoxy. But our relationship with God is neither tied to externals, such as clothing or hair style, nor to a clearly prescribed "pious vocabulary."

4. *A greater emphasis on structures and principles than on persons.* Legalistic religion is largely without compassion and warmth because it causes its adherents to *measure others* rather than enabling them to *meet others* genuinely. Upholding religious principles or codes often becomes an all-consuming passion (recall Paul's zeal in persecuting Christians, considering them enemies of God—Philippians 3:6; Acts 26:9-11). People become "objects" which are evaluated by means of the principles or code; when they do not conform, they are judged and rejected. Relating to them as persons becomes impossible. Such a religious mindset is strikingly illustrated by the story concerning the adulterous woman in the Gospel of John (7:53–8:11). Here, religious codes of morality and the structure of Jewish religion are invoked as a measure for the woman caught in adultery. She becomes a case study, is found wanting, and is therefore expendable: "Let's eliminate her," say the religious purists. But for Jesus the woman is not a case; she is a person in need of restoration and forgiveness. Jesus' own relationship to God provides a framework which allows him to love the adulteress. The religious framework of his opponents is devoid of such a possibility.

5. Closely tied to the last point is a *cold, pious self-righteousness which often manifests itself in a judgmental spirit.* The Gospels are filled with examples of such a religious mentality. Jesus' critics castigated him for associating with the immoral riff-raff of Jewish society, for eating with "known sinners," for caring about Rome's political underlings, the publicans. What is manifested in this criticism is what may be called the "we-they habit" of religion by rules: *we* are righteous, *they* are unrighteous; *we* are good, *they* are bad; *we* are in tune with God, *they* are not; *we* have the truth, *they* do not; *we* interpret the Bible correctly,

they do not. This is what Paul calls "boasting," and it is, according to him, a cardinal sin. The persons who live their lives by external conformity to rules are continually busy attempting "to remove the splinters" from their brothers' and sisters' eyes, without noticing the logjam in their own eyes (see Matthew 7:1-5). The point is clear: self-righteousness is both self-destructive, in that one becomes blind to one's own situation, and it is also destructive of the other person. As such, it is decidedly un-Christian; for the purpose of Christian faith is healing, not destruction.

6. "Religion by rules" is finally characterized by *an inability to respond in joy and spontaneity to situations and to other persons, as well as by a lack of genuine, open love.* The person who is oriented toward rules is always "checking up on himself." Every situation is checked out against a list of "dos" and "don'ts." Every relationship is screened, lest there be defilement. So the religious authorities observed the conduct of Jesus' disciples on a sabbath, checked it off against a list of religious requirements, and found their conduct in violation of "true religion." But Jesus and his disciples had an internal compass which told them that "the sabbath was made for man, not man for the sabbath" (Mark 2:23-27). That is, they responded to a particular human need, knowing that the purpose of God's law is *not to restrict* human existence, *but to enable it.* Or there was the cripple whom Jesus met at a pond in Jerusalem (John 5). The need of the man was overpowering, and Jesus acted in decisive response to that need. But "the righteous" folk whipped out their religious calendar, checked the date, and shouted: "You can't do that today, it's the sabbath!" I recently heard a missionary exuberantly relate how a small band of Christians had gathered early on a Sunday morning for worship and then had spent the rest of the day building a road into the jungle hinterland, in order to reach other tribes with the Good News. I was amazed to hear that certain people had responded by saying that God could not possibly bless such a venture, since it explicitly violated a divine commandment! On the one hand is spontaneous response to human need on the basis of God's love; on the other hand is a calculated invocation of "God's law." The focus has shifted from love and caring to law and judging.

A religion of rules is prohibitive of genuine love, because *objects* cannot receive that kind of love; for when persons are measured and screened, they cease to be persons and become objects. The question confronting a possible relationship is no longer "Is this person in need?" but rather "What is this person's denominational affiliation?" or "Is she a born-again Christian?" or "Does he believe as I do?" or "Is she associated with the World Council of Churches?" A religion of rules creates heresy-hunters, and heresy-hunters are incapable of loving. Love accepts the other in spite of who he or she is. But heresy-hunting rejects the other because of who he or she is. Jesus loved "the sinners" in spite of their sin; but the religious purists rejected "the sinners" because of their sin.

How easy it would be for us to dismiss the kind of counterfeit Christianity described above with the confident affirmation: "But we would never be caught in that trap. That kind of religion is the exclusive property of all those Fundamentalists! Right?" Wrong! For it is this very attitude of "we-they" which blinds us to the fact that a Christian version of Pharisaic legalism is always just around the corner. It is this attitude which brings us precariously close to the brink of practicing some such counterfeit form.

Let us illustrate that danger by means of an example out of Jesus' teaching. In Jesus' parable about the Pharisee and the publican at prayer in the temple (Luke 18:9-14), two contrasting religious attitudes are represented: on the one hand is the haughty, self-righteous Pharisee; on the other is the outright, self-confessed sinner. In reading the parable, *we immediately identify with the publican.* What we are saying with this identification is really this: "God, I thank you that I am not like this Pharisee!" With that we have almost unwittingly fallen into the neat little trap which Jesus set. The whole point of the parable is that humility, not arrogance, is our proper stance before God and in relation to our fellow human beings.

Christian existence is existence at the crossroads:.
between religion which *enslaves us* to ourselves
    and religion which *frees us* from ourselves;
between religion which *separates us* from the other
    and religion which *sets us free* for the other;
between religion which *entices us to judge* the other
    and religion which *empowers us to love* the other;
between religion which *closes us off* from the world
    and religion which *prepares us to face* the world;
between religion which *molds us into external conformity*
    and religion which *elicits joyful commitment and allegiance.*
In Romans 7, Paul has demonstrated that even religiously committed and zealous persons, despite affirmations of orthodoxy, demonstrations of piety, and right knowledge about

moral requirements, are constantly threatened by a performance gap. Somehow the religious person's *potential* falls short of actualization. Somehow in the quest to secure an acceptable place before God, one becomes ultimately a slave to his or her own efforts.

In light of the fact that even religion can land a person in that kind of a dilemma and in light of the fact that all of us stand in the desert of decision between a form of Christianity which enslaves and a form which sets free, what guarantees that the *new freedom* for the *new obedience* can find actualization? What guarantees that the new freedom will not inevitably come to naught in another performance gap? What guarantees that our *potential for the new obedience* can find concrete realization?

Chapter 8 of Romans supplies the answer to these questions: It is the gift of the presence of the life-giving Spirit (8:2) which guarantees that the new life of freedom does not inevitably end up on the trash heap of another performance gap. It is that Presence which assures that the new life is not characterized by despair at failure, cynical frustration, utter weakness.

It is the presence of the Spirit which moves Christian existence *from impotence to a new potency.* It is the presence of the Spirit which empowers us *to move from a state of freedom for the new obedience* to daily *incarnation of that obedience.* It is the presence of the Spirit which lifts us, again and again, as we live in radical openness before God and our fellow human beings, *out of the realm of religious captivity into the light and joy of religious freedom.*

Questions for Reflection

1. Reflect on and share the kind of enslavements from which God's love frees us.
2. What would a truly free and freeing life-style look like?
3. The gift of freedom and the continuing reality of those things which want to enslave us confront each other in our Christian lives. What is the cause of such confrontation, and how can we deal creatively with it?
4. Discuss ways in which religious practice, piety, devotion can enslave us. How can Christian faith free us from such religious captivity?

CHAPTER 5

Between Myself and Other "Selves"

It is hardly an accident that Paul climaxes his Letter to the Romans with what is commonly considered to be the *practical* or *ethical* section. Indeed, the regular pattern of the epistle falls into two balanced sections: (1) A "theological" section, which consists of an exposition of the gospel, the Good News. We have been speaking of that Good News in terms of the *creation of the new situation and its possibility.* (2) An "ethical" section, which lays down the principles for the kind of Christian life-style demanded by that new situation. For when all is said and done, the question which invariably presses itself upon us is this: what difference does the event of justification make in terms of the "nuts and bolts" of everyday living with our fellow human beings?

Let us recall that the working hypothesis undergirding the foregoing series of studies has been that the divine intention in the salvation event is *the restoration of the divine-human relationship.* If that is correct, then there is but one sphere in which that restored divine-human relationship can come to expression and can bear fruit. That one sphere is the sphere of human relationships, whether that be (1) between the individual and the community (Romans 12–13) or (2) between individuals in the context of inter-personal relationships (Romans 14–15:13).

Christians are persons who are always—potentially and in faith—members of a New Humanity. They stand always—potentially and in faith—on the threshold of a new possibility. This new possibility consists of the freedom to live before God in such a way that his relationship-restoring love for us becomes incarnated in a relationship-restoring love between ourselves and others.

To be living, therefore, within *the magnetic field of the New Humanity* means that our living moves increasingly toward the realization of the *model* provided by Him who is the Head of that New Humanity.

Jesus was, in the deepest sense, "the Man for others." And it was in that sense that he was most fully and most genuinely human. He was the "authentic human being"—and thus the counterpart of the "first Adam" (1 Corinthians 15:45)—in that *he was there for others in freedom and love!*

So it is that Paul brings his epistle to a conclusion by showing that it is in the sphere of personal relationships where the "new possibility" is put to its most stringent test. For if it does not prove itself there, then any and all claims to *piety*, to *devotion*, to *orthodoxy in belief* are nothing more than a "noisy gong or a clanging cymbal" (1 Corinthians 13:1).

A detailed interpretation of the wealth of insight which meets us in these last chapters of Romans is not within the purview of this essay. We will simply attempt to gain some perspectives which will enable us to come to grips with the tensions which arise in the conflict between the individual and the larger community and between individuals in the context of interpersonal relationships.

In light of our contention throughout these chapters that the New Testament (and specifically Paul) does not permit a splitting of the person into a *higher* and *lower self* or a division between the physical and the spiritual, it is highly significant that Paul begins in chapter 12 by speaking of the *renewal of the mind*. With the affirmation of this necessity, he drives at the heart of the misunderstanding of so many of his contemporaries, for whom the "mind" was that higher part of man which was most in tune with God. Often, the words "spirit" and "soul" were used to designate that higher part of man. By talking about the renewal of the mind, Paul's point is that it is at the core of our being, namely in our *willing*, our *deciding*, our *motivation*, that God's reorientation of us must find expression. This is what Paul means by the phrase, "present your bodies as a living sacrifice" (12:1). That is, our *concrete existence*, in its *total orientation*, is to be determined by the fact that God is at work reclaiming his creation and that the Christian is called upon to be a participant in that renewing and reclaiming process.

There is an important perspective which emerges out of Paul's use of the language of the cult ("present your bodies a living sacrifice") at this point in his letter. This is so in view of the fact that (1) cultic language is virtually absent from Paul's letters and (2) Christianity was the only religion in antiquity without a cult—that is, without priests, temples, shrines, and sacrifices that were separated from the realm of the secular. For Christianity there was no division between the sacred and the profane. The close association between the "love feast" (a fellowship meal) and the celebration of the Lord's Supper in the early church is a good example of the refusal to separate cult from life. What is important, says Paul, is not that we *set apart* certain things for the service of God, such as certain hours on particular days or a percentage of our incomes or specific talents or abilities. What is important is that *all of life becomes sacralized,* that *all of life comes to stand under the lordship of Christ,* that *all of life is a transforming and healing presence* in the midst of the world. It is simply impossible—on the basis of this Pauline perspective—to affirm the Pauline gospel but to cop out at the point where it impinges upon human relationships. Faith and life cannot be held in isolated compartments; they must intersect.

There is an insightful passage in C. S. Lewis' *Screwtape Letters* which illustrates the matter quite strikingly. In a correspondence from Screwtape to Wormwood, one of his demonic underlings who is in charge of a recent convert to Christianity, the following advice is given:

> The great thing is to direct the malice to his immediate neighbours whom he meets every day and to thrust his benevolence out to the remote circumference, to people he does not know. The malice thus becomes wholly real and the benevolence largely imaginary.[1]

"I love mankind, it's people I can't stand," is the way it appears in life. Insofar as we as Christians can conjure up devotion and love for faraway people without at the same time bringing that devotion and love to bear on our immediate and close relationships, the demonic is in control in our lives. The point is quite clear: Christian devotion, worship, giving, and believing, if not exercised with respect to and in the context of concrete and specific human relationships, are really demonic!

It is demonic to claim to have love for God and hate those who are against us (Romans 12:14, 17, 19-21). And how alive that kind of dichotomy is in many quarters of American Christianity. A comment heard on a San Francisco radio station conveys such a perverted sentiment quite well:

> Violence has no place in America! Anyone who preaches violence should be shot like a dog![2]

It is demonic to give money for "the salvation of black souls" in Africa, and to move out of the neighborhood when one of their race moves in next door!

It is demonic to claim the forgiveness of God for our own lives and to continue to pass judgment on our brothers or sisters at the same time (Romans 14:3-4). The entire New Testament is clear on that point. In the Lord's Prayer the forgiveness of God in our lives stands in direct proportion to our willingness to forgive (Matthew 6:12). And John is decisive at the point of the direct correspondence between the *vertical relationship* (ourselves and God) and the *horizontal relationship* (ourselves and others)—1 John 2:7-11; 4:7-12).

It is demonic to rejoice in our Christian freedom from the bondage to law (external requirements) and at the same time to despise those who have not become free from such bondage (Romans 14:3f; 15:1-2).

It is demonic to live that Christian freedom in such a way that our brothers or sisters are shattered by it rather than made whole (Romans 14:13-20).

It is demonic to claim the freedom for which Christ has set us free and yet to live a Christian version of Pharisaic legalism which causes us to pass judgment upon those who are really free from those legalisms (Romans 14:1-9).

Both because of the possibility of the kind of "double standard" indicated above and because of the demonic nature of such a double standard, Paul seeks to broaden the focus from the examination of personal restoration into the exploration of human relationships. And immediately we are confronted by phrases and admonitions in the text (Romans 12–15) which bring into focus two of the most troublesome areas of tension for Christian existence: (1) the tension created in the confrontation between our individual rights and needs and our responsibility in regard to the rights and needs of the community; (2) the tension created in the confrontation between our own needs and the needs of other individuals.

A selective listing of the textual material will help us to focus on these areas of tension. (In some cases, a free rendering of the substance of the text is given):

> 12:3 . . . I bid every one among you
> not to think of himself more
> highly than he ought to think. . . .
> 12:5 We are one body in Christ and
> individually members of it.
> 12:16 Live in harmony with one
> another; do not be haughty,
> but associate with the lowly. . . .
> 12:18 . . . live peaceably with all.
> 13:1 Let every person be subject
> to the governing authorities. . . .
> 13:8 Owe no one anything,
> except to love one another. . . .
> 14:1 Welcome him who is weak
> in faith.
> 14:7 None of us lives to himself. . . .
> 14:15 If your brother is injured
> by your actions, you are
> not walking in love.
> 14:19 Let us then pursue what makes
> for peace and for mutual
> upbuilding.
> 15:1 We who are strong ought to bear
> with the failings of the weak,
> and not to please ourselves.

This list of admonitions is climaxed in what is really the heart of the entire discussion:

15:7 Welcome one another, therefore, as Christ has welcomed you. . . .

The Greek word behind the RSV's "welcome" is perhaps better translated with "accept." The meaning is, of course, that God's acceptance of us, while we were rebels (Romans 5:8) is the basis for a "despite" kind of relatedness to our fellow human beings. In terms of the structure of Paul's argument in Romans, one can hardly fail to recognize the connection between the first part of the letter and these closing chapters. In chapters 1:18–2:29 a humanity which stands under the judgment of God is depicted: it is a humanity characterized by deceit, perversion, bitterness, rejection, alienation. God breaks into that humanity with his relationship-restoring love.

Now Paul's admonitions in chapters 12–15 presuppose a situation in the Christian community in Rome where divisiveness, interpersonal alienation, and the manifestation of a judgmental spirit threaten the health of both individuals and the community. To that situation Paul speaks a decisive word: *out of the indicative of God's restoration of us follows the imperative for our restoration of our neighbor.* Our action toward our fellow human beings is to be nothing less than the extension of God's action toward us.

Let us briefly look at the significance of this affirmation for the tension between the individual and the larger community or other individuals in three areas: (1) the community of faith; (2) the human community; (3) the family (as the sphere of intense interpersonal relationships).

The Community of Faith

The discussion in Romans 12 centers on the affirmation that ". . . we, though many, are one body in Christ, and individually members one of another" (12:5). What does it mean to be an individual in that mix?

I would like to get at an answer to that question through a comparison of two biblical affirmations concerning humankind and nature, respectively.

> When I look at thy heavens, the work of thy fingers,
>   the moon and the stars which thou hast established;
> what is man that thou art mindful of him. . . ?
> Yet thou hast made him little less than God,
>   and dost crown him with glory and honor.
>
> (Psalm 8:3-5)
>
> The heavens are telling the glory of God;
>   and the firmament proclaims his handiwork.
> Day to day pours forth speech,
>   and night to night declares knowledge.
> There is no speech, nor are there words;
>   their voice is not heard;
> yet their voice goes out through all the earth,
>   and their words to the end of the world.
>
> (Psalm 19:1-4)

Here we have two great texts from the Old Testament. On the one hand is a picture of a person who, over against the macrocosm, fades into an insignificant microcosmic speck. Yet there is also the astounding affirmation that this speck of dust is the crown of God's creation: humankind is but a little less than God, crowned with glory and honor, with dominion over the rest of the created order.

On the other hand is a picture of the created universe which exists as a sign, pointing beyond itself in a mysterious and inexplicable way to the power and glory and majesty of God the Creator.

The biblical point of view affirms that the created order *reflects God.* Though muted and eternally silent, it communicates the reality of God in a nonverbal way. But the biblical point of view also affirms that the human being, created in God's image and thus a natural candidate for the reflection process, refuses to fulfill its function.

What does it mean to be created in God's image (Genesis 1:27) and thus to be in a position to reflect the glory of God? The theological discussions throughout the history of the church give a number of suggestions: human reason, creativity, freedom, power are among the prime candidates for that in humankind which qualifies us for the designation "image of God." But in what sense have we, by these means, reflected the glory and majesty of God? Indeed, we have used these distinguishing traits of humankind as instruments for chaos rather than order, for destruction rather than life, for hate rather than love, for disintegration rather than wholeness.

Some time ago I stood on the observation deck of one of the skyscrapers in Chicago, looking out over the skyline of that great city. I could not help but be impressed by that scene which reflected the genius, the creativity, the resourcefulness, the power of humanity. But as I reflected upon what I saw, I became painfully aware that below me lay also the scene of the infamous Chicago riots; and to the west and south sprawled the ghettos of human misery and frustration and rejection as signposts on the human landscape, pointing to the reality of brokenness in human relationships.

What does it mean to be created in God's image?

> So God created man in his own image, in the image of God he created him; male and female he created them (Genesis 1:27).

The creation of "Adam" (humankind)[3] in the image of God is further defined in the second part of the verse by the male-female duality. This means that the concept of the "image of God" does not refer to the human being as an isolated individual, but to the human being insofar as that human being is in relationship with another human being. That is to say, the "image of God" is present and realizes itself as human beings are related to one another in keeping with the intention of the Creator. Emil Brunner expressed it beautifully when he wrote that the human being "cannot realize his nature without the 'Other'; his destiny is fellowship in love."[4]

Such an understanding of *existence-in-community* as the medium through which the glory of God is reflected must be seen as the background for Paul's understanding of the Christian community as "one body in Christ" (Romans 12:5; or "body of Christ"—1 Corinthians 12:27). It is hardly accidental that Paul speaks of Christ as the one "who is the likeness of God" (2 Corinthians 4:4). He is the True Person. He fulfills in himself the purpose of human existence *in that he is there for others.* He came to live out, in the context of human relationships, the "image of God." In him, says John the evangelist, we have seen and experienced the steadfast love and faithfulness of God (see John 1:14).

Paul not only affirms that Christ is the image of God, but also that Christians are those who are "being changed into his image." Therefore, to be transformed into the image of Christ, who truly reflects the image of God, means that we must increasingly translate and transmute Christ's restoring love for us into the arena of our daily relationships. To be "in Christ," for Paul, is synonymous with "to be in the church." And existence "in the church" means participation in a community in which healing and wholeness can happen because the individuals within it are truly there for each other.

That is why Paul uses the analogy of the "body" in speaking of the nature of the Christian fellowship. It is an organism in which the various parts work harmoniously toward a common purpose (12:3-17). But do we really know what it means to be a body? One look at what much of church life looks like would warrant a negative answer to that question.

I cannot speak for other Christian traditions, but my participation in Baptist fellowships has convinced me that we Baptists are quite an individualistic lot. In Baptist confessions, church covenants, and manuals of polity and practice, one is confronted by phrases and concepts which indicate this individualistic strain: liberty of conscience; private interpretation of Scripture; priesthood of believers; etc. The historical roots of this individualism are clear. It emerged out of both the rejection of ecclesiastical authority and the rejection of coercion in matters of faith and worship by governmental authority. But the consciousness of these historical reasons was gradually supplanted by the invasion of an American "rugged individualism": no one tells me; I do my own thing.

It seems that the arena of church business meetings often reflects such an individualistic understanding of the nature of the church. We operate with the underlying notion that the church is a democracy, that therefore the majority rules, and that "Roberts'

Rules of Order" is the bible for the church's conduct of business. That is at best a misunderstanding of the nature of the Christian community. A church is no more a democracy than a platoon of soldiers engaged on a specific mission or a football team on the field. Is it possible to equate the lordship of Christ (who is the Head of the body, the church) with the will of the majority? Hardly! For the problem with "majority rule," of course, is that the majority may be wrong. In fact, the principle of majority rule in the church may be decidedly un-Christian. Majority rule makes it possible to join other individuals whose self-interest is the same as ours, and to outvote all those whose interests and needs conflict with ours. So in church business meetings we really often lord it over our brothers and sisters by means of majority vote; that is, we crush the others.

Certainly, *consensus* as a means for the decision-making process of the church is a much more difficult procedure than majority rule. But it is a procedure clearly implied, if not demanded, by the nature of the church as the body of Christ. And *consensus,* under the guidance of the Spirit of Christ, is clearly the means by which the early Christian communities carried on their work: ". . . it has seemed good to the Holy Spirit and to us . . ." (Acts 15:28).

Working toward consensus and unanimity in the affairs of the local congregation will clearly demand more patience, more sensitivity toward each other's needs, and a deeper openness to the demands of the mind of Christ than are often demonstrated at church business meetings. But the result—in terms of the creation of a community in which healing and wholeness can happen—is certainly worth the effort. The alternative is nothing less than disintegration and fragmentation.

The "body" which operates by majority rule opens itself inevitably to disease. When a rationally conceived course of action, such as the attainment of a goal or the achievement of an ideal, is supported by our willful determination in disregard for the need of our bodies for rest, the road toward the body's disintegration is beginning to be paved. This is especially the case if reason and will continue to outvote the legitimate needs of the physical dimension. Medical science has clearly shown that such an *existence by majority vote* has caused the plight of many heart attack victims. It is also true that an existence dominated by the conjunction of physical appetites and a reinforcing volition, in opposition to the recognition of higher human strivings, is headed toward internal fragmentation and personal destruction.

The analogy of this state of affairs to the dynamics that are operative in the "body-life" of the Christian fellowship can hardly be missed. If love is going to be genuine (12:9), then it will not do for us simply to join ourselves to others who are likeminded and outvote our brothers and sisters whose convictions and ideas are not in concert with ours. The task is rather, in the context of genuine love, for both the "majority" and the "minority" to confront one another, to hear one another, to affirm one another, and finally to move into territory which they can occupy with one another. This process does not demand the loss of integrity for either side; neither loses, both win. What the process does demand is the will to harmony (12:16), respect for the other (12:10), acceptance of diversity (12:4-8), and humility with respect to one's own stature (12:3, 16).

Christians are persons who are always potentially part of a new created order. They are free before God and their fellow human beings to reflect the glory of God in an existence-for-the-other. One area in which this potential can find actualization is the Christian fellowship, the local congregation. It is high time that we put the "image of God" to the test in that fellowship!

The Human Community

In chapter 13 of Romans, Paul focuses on the tension between the individual and society at large in terms of the problem of civil obedience or disobedience. The question which is raised concerns the individual's responsibility toward the social order, insofar as that social order is regulated by laws which are upheld and enforced by government authorities.

We live in a day in which this tension has come to the fore in this nation. There is the question of civil disobedience in respect to "bad" laws; there is the question of granting amnesty to those who evaded the draft on the grounds that the Vietnam conflict was immoral or that our participation in it was illegal. On the other hand is the whole problem of what is called "civil religion," in which patriotism, often of a quite unconditional type, is clothed with a mantle of religious respectability.

How do Christians deal with the tension created by their presence in a society in which the need to preserve their integrity as individuals and to be faithful to their understanding of the lordship of Christ may conflict with the demands of that society?

Senator Mark O. Hatfield, in his Preface to a series of essays published in *The Cross and the Flag*, asserts that "Christians often have rendered unto Caesar that which is God's."[5] He goes on to show, by means of a series of contrasting scriptural passages, that individual Christian responsibility has often been compromised on the basis of a one-sided use of biblical injunctions. Thus, Romans 13 and 1 Peter 2:13-14 are cited as proof that the state always demands and deserves our total and unquestioning obedience. But Revelation 13 and 18 are neglected; the former pictures the state as a beast, the latter speaks of the downfall of any nation which becomes a modern Babylon, corrupted by its wealth, materialism, and injustice.

Some persons are quick to condemn any person who upsets or threatens to upset social normalcy. But those same Christians disregard the text in Acts 17:6-7 where the apostles are described as "men who have turned the world upside down" and who "are all acting against the decrees of Caesar, saying that there is another king, Jesus."

It is also clear from the Gospel accounts of Jesus' ministry that he did not accept all legal and governing authorities as ultimate dispensers of God's will. Wherever he went, he bucked the system, he upset the status quo, he challenged the authorities' claim to the right and the truth.[6] And in the context of a life of discipleship, countless martyrs throughout the history of the Christian era gave their lives because they resisted the decrees of the authorities.

Thus, a serious look at the scriptural material will prevent us from viewing the demands of society and its rulers with uncritical acceptance and automatic approval. There are conditions when the demands of the social order must be resisted and the worth of the individual as a responsible being before God must be affirmed and defended.

Dietrich Bonhoeffer, at the end of a hangman's noose, paid the price of actively resisting the decrees of the Nazi regime.[7] Karl Barth was exiled from his native Germany because he refused to sign a document, required of all university professors, that gave absolute and unquestioning obedience and allegiance to the Führer. There were many, both among the membership and the leadership of the church in Germany, who, on the basis of an uncritical acceptance of Romans 13 and 1 Peter 2:13, refused to join the *Confessing Church* movement and remained silent.

Which of these groups was more in tune with God's will? To suggest, as I have heard it suggested, that Bonhoeffer and others in the Resistance movement got what they deserved for disobeying the injunctions of Romans 13 is surely the grossest kind of perverted interpretation of God's Word and will. Or again, to suggest that God used Hitler to punish the Jews for their rejection of the Messiah and that therefore the mass murder of millions of them was part of his plan is to betray a total insensitivity to the God who confronts persons in Jesus and asks them to come home to himself!

Whereas we simply cannot give uncritical and unquestioning allegiance to the demands of society and its governing authorities, we must also be careful not to go to the other extreme: that of concluding that government is inevitably an evil institution that should be resisted, disobeyed, distrusted, or ignored. For we are instructed to honor and pray for those in authority, and the biblical witness makes clear that there is a design for a positive role for government to play in the fulfillment of God's intention for human existence in community. According to the New Testament, all authority is ultimately under the rule and judgment of Christ.

In light of this double perspective, how are we to understand Romans 13, which seems, especially on a superficial reading, to come down on one side of this double perspective? First, we need to read Romans 13 more carefully than it has often been read. Second, we need to read these admonitions in light of the context of Paul's missionary activity, which took place in a world in which Roman law and rule had created relative peace and order, conducive to the rapid spread of the gospel.

Let us carefully follow, in outline form, the argument of Paul:

> *Statement:* "Let every person be subject to the governing authorities" (13:1).
>
> *Hypothetical Question:* Why?
>
> *Answer:* Because all authority exists ultimately by God's design, including the authority of the state (see 13:1*b*).
>
> *Conclusion:* Therefore, to resist the authorities is to resist the intention of God (see 13:2).
>
> *Hypothetical Question:* But what is the intention of God?
>
> *Answer:* It is the intention of God that, through his "servants" (governing authorities),
>
> —evil acts are punished (see 12:4),
>
> —bad works are restrained through fear of punishment (see 12:3*a*),
>
> —the good is promoted and encouraged (see 12:3*b*).

In summary, Paul's argument is this: It is God's intention that human life in the context of community will be life in harmony and peace (see 12:10, 18) and order. And since life in community becomes chaotic and anarchistic without the presence of regulatory laws which are enforced by rulers, governors, and lawmakers, the presence of these and their authority are part of the overall intention of God for human existence.

> *Conclusion:* Therefore, insofar as the state and its rulers exercise their authority *in keeping with the intention of God,* they act as God's ministers for the common good of society.

If, however, the authority of the state runs counter to this divine intention, then there is no reason why that authority should be understood as God-given. In fact, it becomes quite clear from Revelation 13 and 18, as well as other places in the New Testament, that the state which persecutes Christians, which dispenses injustice instead of justice, which supports moral decay, which tramples on the weak and powerless, has been usurped by demonic powers and forces which are diametrically opposed to God's purposes and intentions.

The passage which follows Paul's discussion about the relationship between the individual and the demands of the social order (13:8-10) is very instructive for a proper understanding of that relationship. Most commentators feel that Paul has completed the considerations about obedience to the state and is now speaking about morality and ethics in general. It seems to me, however, that such an understanding of the thrust of the argument overlooks the very specific intention of Paul at this particular point.

Indeed, the admonitions concerning love for the other in verses 8-10 are not a departure from the previous topic, but are rather a climax of the entire discussion. Verse 8 picks up very pointedly from the previous verse. There, the argument for obedience to state and for responsible existence within the social order, is driven home in terms of specific things that we owe: taxes, respect, honor. But beyond these specifics, Paul goes on to argue (vv. 8-9) that what we really owe is to love others even as we love ourselves.

According to Paul's heritage, the authorities in government are really intended to be guardians of the commandments which make life in community possible, namely:

> do not kill,
> do not steal,
> do not commit adultery,
> etc.

Each of these, if violated, lead to destruction and fragmentation of community. Since the law is summed up in the commandment, "You shall love your neighbor as yourself" (v. 9), the loving of one's fellow human beings—not doing any wrong to them—"is the fulfilling of the law" (v. 10). It is responsibility for both the protection and the enforcing of this law which is given to human authorities by the design of God.

What if, in our expression of love to our fellow human beings, we run smack into the laws of the society in which we live? What if the rulers act in opposition to their intended purpose as stated in 13:3? What if they become a terror to the good? What if the demands of the social order require us to be molded into a life-style which is contrary to the implicit and explicit demands of the gospel?

There are no pat answers to these questions. Anyone who suggests easy solutions or indeed *the Christian response* has simply failed to understand the complexities of the world in which we find ourselves and has disregarded the reality that each of us perceives that world through personally-tinted glasses. Nonetheless, we must become increasingly sensitive to the issues raised by these questions and must respond in keeping with our understanding of the call of Christ. And that call is decisively a call to be there for the other in love. If we fail at this point, even the most carefully woven cloth of orthodox belief and pious practice will finally become nothing but a tattered rag!

The Family as the Sphere of Intense Interpersonal Relationships

In Romans 14, Paul comes to grips with a very practical situation in the life of the Christian community. There are those whose faith commitments are more or less tied to external restraints, whose Christian life-style is somewhat determined by external conformity to codes of conduct. In conflict with these are Christians who have come to understand that the way of faith is the way of freedom; that externals, such as "imbibing certain foods or liquids," do not affect one's relationship with God. The former are the "weak in faith" (14:1). The latter, by implication, are the "strong in faith."

Either stance, says Paul, becomes dangerous when it becomes the norm for evaluating the "Christian commitment" of the other. The one becomes the basis for a judgmental spirit; the other leads to haughtiness (14:3). In either case there is alienation and *de*struction, rather than peace and *con*struction (14:13-19).

The principle by which Paul evaluates the situation is strikingly annunciated in 14:17:

> . . . the kingdom of God is not food and drink but righteousness and peace and joy in the Holy Spirit.

Let us briefly analyze this principle. The idea of the "kingdom of God," which appears so frequently in the teaching ministry of Jesus, is not to be understood in geographical, spatial terms, but rather as a dynamic reality: the reign of God as it manifests itself in concrete human experience. That dynamic reality, says Paul, has nothing whatever to do with what we eat or drink. Rather, the fruit of God's reign in our lives—as we are open to the Spirit's mediation of that reign—is evidenced in terms of *righteousness, peace, joy.*

These three words get at the heart of the meaning and purpose of Christian existence. If we take seriously the Pauline understanding of *God's righteousness* as his *relationship-restoring love,* then the fruit of that in our lives is a manifestation of relationship-restoring love toward those with whom we exist. "Peace" is the opposite of war or alienation. Peace is the condition of a relationship where the enmity is gone. Peace means *acceptance.* Thus, the fruit of God's acceptance of us (Romans 5:1) comes to concrete expression in our acceptance of the other. "Joy," wherever it appears in the New Testament, has to do with *deep satisfaction,* with *purposeful existence,* with *wholeness.* So Paul's response to the recognition of the restoration of the Creator-creature relationship is the response of joy (Romans 5:2, 11). Only joy, as an expression of purposiveness and wholeness, can withstand the pressures of external adversity (Romans 5:3; Philippians). God's reign in us creates purpose, direction, and wholeness; the fruit of that is being there for the other in such a way that wholeness also becomes a part of his or her experience.

The New Testament leaves no doubt as to where the "kingdom of God" was most deeply modeled; namely in Jesus of Nazareth. Wherever and whenever God's reign touched people's lives during Jesus' ministry, they experienced the reality of forgiveness; they became aware of God's love and grace; they were lifted out of loneliness and despair; they were freed from the bondage to things and to self; they were given a new purpose and a new meaning for living. The broken were restored to wholeness; the skeptics were led to trust God; the despised and rejected of humanity were given new worth; the wrecks of humanity found healing.

Jesus called his disciples to become an extension of that presence of God's reign. What Jesus gave to the world was a little band of extremely common people whose total impact was miraculous. Though the members of this tiny group of disciples were individually unworthy, the fellowship which they came to share was so tremendous that the redemption, the healing, the forgiveness of Jesus continued to be realized wherever these disciples reflected in their living and sharing something of the reign of God.

What is the significance of this original Christian story for the Christian family as a small band of disciples? It is in the recognition that the family—though the individual members be weak and unworthy—can be a fellowship which reflects the presence of God's reign, can be a foretaste of God's kingdom,[8] can be, as it were, *the kingdom of God in miniature.*

The family, as the sphere of intense interpersonal relationships, must be the primary testing ground for the reality of relationship-restoring and relationship-building love. It must be the primary testing ground for the acceptance of one another, with all our diversities, on the basis of grace. It must be the primary testing ground for the possibility of joy in the midst of the very natural tensions and stresses of the home.

Our families can become kingdoms of God in miniature:
> when living faith is more caught than taught, because it is the unstated groundwork, the foundation of all that is said and done;
>
> when love is freely given and unselfishly shared;
>
> when forgiving one another becomes as natural as eating and sleeping;
>
> when we accept one another as we are and refuse the attempt to mold the other in keeping with one's own image;
>
> when we do not use and abuse one another.

As kingdoms of God in miniature, our homes can become places of potential healing and restoration. The individual members may return to them from the storms of the world for understanding and strength. From them they may go out to be God's people in the world. The many ideologies and movements and causes in our world put tremendous pressure upon our youth, claiming their allegiance. They need homes in which, no matter how great their frustrations and disappointments, they can become new people because there is firm but loving guidance; because there is a willingness to listen and to understand and to affirm and to forgive.

To what extent do our homes reflect these characteristics of the kingdom? Are they places in which the healing and love of Christ are tested and demonstrated? Are they places where genuine sharing of one another's successes and failures takes place? Or are they simply houses in which we may perhaps *live with one another* out of economic or biological necessity, but in which there is *no living for one another?*

We are intended for existence-in-love and existence-in-community. There can hardly be a better proving ground for the possibility of that kind of existence than the family. The movement from the indicative of God's acceptance of us to the imperative of our acceptance of each other must begin there. If it does not happen there, it will likely happen nowhere else.

Questions for Reflection

1. We were created to be there for others. If we really took this truth seriously, how could it find expression in our individual relationships and in our congregational life?
2. Think of ways (besides those given in the preceding chapter) in which the demonic expresses itself in our human relationships. (The purpose of this exercise is to discover how subtly the demonic infiltrates our living.)
3. What implications for our living does the following statement have: there is no distinction between the "sacred" and the "secular" in Christian perspective.
4. In our society, where do the demands of the lordship of Christ come into conflict with the demands of that society? How do we preserve our integrity and remain faithful? How are "Cross" and "Flag" related to one another?

Notes

Introduction

[1] Blaise Pascal, cited in Os Guinness, *The Dust of Death* (Downers Grove, Ill.: InterVarsity Press, 1973), p. 2.

Chapter 1

[1] William Sanday and Arthur C. Headlam, *A Critical and Exegetical Commentary on the Epistle to the Romans*, The International Critical Commentary (New York: Charles Scribner's Sons, 1929), p. 36.

[2] Norman H. Snaith, *The Distinctive Ideas of the Old Testament* (Philadelphia: The Westminster Press, 1966), pp. 207-222.

[3] "Diaspora Jews" were those living outside Palestine throughout the Hellenistic world. "God-fearers" were Gentiles who had adopted the Jewish faith with its lofty monotheism, but who had not submitted to the Jewish rituals, particularly circumcision.

[4] See the discussion concerning Paul's educational upbringing in W. C. Van Unnik, *Tarsus or Jerusalem: The City of Paul's Youth*, trans. George Ogg (London: The Epworth Press, 1962).

[5] The RSV translates "victory" where we have rendered "salvation" and "vindication" where we have rendered "righteousness." The translators gave the meaning of the text; but for the purposes of our study it is better to render that text more literally.

[6] The translation of the Scrolls is that given by Geza Vermes, in *The Dead Sea Scrolls in English* (Baltimore: Penguin Books, 1962), pp. 163-164.

[7] *Ibid.*, p. 198.

[8] *Ibid.*, p. 193.

[9] The RSV renders the Greek word *adikia* with "wickedness" in all three texts. This is unfortunate, since it immediately introduces the ethical-moral understanding into these verses. It is better to preserve the parallelism between the term "righteousness" and "unrighteousness" as in the Greek text (*dikaiosune* and *adikia*).

94

[10] Taken from *The Literature of England*, ed. George K. Anderson and William E. Buckler (Glenville, Ill.: Scott, Foresman and Company, 1966), p. 1397.

[11] St. Augustine, "Great Art Thou, O Lord," *Masterpieces of Religious Verse*, ed., James Dalton Morrison (New York: Harper & Row, Publishers, 1948), p. 65.

[12] Dean M. Kelley, *Why Conservative Churches Are Growing* (New York: Harper & Row, Publishers, 1972).

Chapter 2

[1] Os Guinness, *The Dust of Death* (Downers Grove, Ill.: InterVarsity Press, 1973). See also Clarence A. Glasrud, *The Age of Anxiety* (Boston: Houghton Mifflin Company, 1960).

[2] Francis A. Schaeffer, *Pollution and the Death of Man. The Christian View of Ecology* (Wheaton, Ill.: Tyndale House Publishers, 1970).

[3] H. Wheeler Robinson, *Corporate Personality in Ancient Israel* (Philadelphia: Fortress Press, 1964).

[4] Second Esdras, in *The New Oxford Annotated Bible with the Apocrypha*, eds. Herbert G. May and Bruce M. Metzger (New York: Oxford University Press, 1973), pp. 27, 28, 42.

[5] Martin Bell, *The Way of the Wolf. The Gospel in New Images* (New York: The Seabury Press, Inc., 1970), p. 83.

[6] Os Guinness, *op. cit.*, p. 2, quoting Carl Jung, "Epilogue," *Modern Man in Search of a Soul* (New York: Routledge Books, 1933).

[7] The Hebrew word is *nephesh*, and it is more accurate to translate with the word "person." The word "soul" introduces a Greek idea which is not present in the Hebrew term.

[8] The Wisdom of Solomon, in *The Apocrypha* (New York: Thomas Nelson & Sons, 1957), pp. 87, 88.

[9] Second Baruch, in R. H. Charles, *The Apocrypha and Pseudepigrapha of the Old Testament*, vol. 2 (Oxford: The Clarendon Press, 1913), p. 512.

[10] See Karl Menninger, *Whatever Became of Sin?* (New York: Hawthorn Books, Inc., 1973), pp. 22-23.

[11] William Glasser, *Reality Therapy* (New York: Harper & Row, Publishers, 1965).

[12] Paul is not precise in his use of the impersonal pronouns "all" and "many." The list shows that he uses the terms interchangeably. Paul is concerned to point out the connection between first man and the rest of humankind.

[13] These statements cannot be used either for the theory of limited atonement or of universalism (see note 12 above).

Chapter 3

[1] See Jacques Ellul, *The Technological Society*, trans. J. Wilkinson (New York: Alfred A. Knopf, Inc., 1964).

[2] Adolf Deissmann, *Paul, a Study in Social and Religious History* (London: Hodder and Stoughton, 1926), pp. 149-157.

[3]C. S. Lewis, *The Screwtape Letters* (New York: The Macmillan Company, 1944), pp. 20-22.

[4]*Ibid.,* p. 17.

Chapter 4

[1]See the excellent discussion of this matter in W. D. Davies, *Invitation to the New Testament* (London: Darton, Longman & Todd Ltd., 1967), pp. 274-277.

[2]Solomon Schechter gives a good description of the Jewish understanding of the law in *Aspects of Rabbinic Theology* (New York: Schocken Books, Inc., 1961), pp. 148-169.

[3]*The Baptist Herald,* vol. 52, (February, 1974), p. 30.

Chapter 5

[1]C. S. Lewis, *The Screwtape Letters* (New York: The Macmillan Company, 1944), p. 37.

[2]Quoted in Os Guinness, *The Dust of Death* (Downers Grove, Ill.: InterVarsity Press, 1973), p. 150.

[3]Old Testament scholarship has pretty clearly shown that the tradition reflected in Genesis 1:27 understands "Adam" in generic terms. That is, both "man" and "woman" are included in the designation "Adam." This is unequivocally stated in Genesis 5:2—"Male and female he created them, and he blessed them and named them Man [Adam] when they were created." (I am indebted here to the insights of my colleague in Old Testament, Dr. Reidar Bjornard). Cf. Gerhard von Rad, *Genesis: A Commentary,* trans. John H. Marks (Philadelphia: The Westminster Press, 1961), p. 55.

[4]Emil Brunner, *The Christian Doctrine of Creation and Redemption* (Philadelphia: The Westminster Press, 1952), p. 64.

[5]Robert Clouse, Robert Linder, and Richard Pierard, eds., *The Cross and the Flag* (Carol Stream, Ill.: Creation House, 1972), p. 9.

[6]See the group Bible study guide by Ada Lum, *Jesus the Radical* (Downers Grove, Ill.: InterVarsity Press, 1972).

[7]The biblical foundation for Bonhoeffer's stance is laid in his *The Cost of Discipleship* (New York: The Macmillan Company, 1959).

[8]Elton Trueblood, *The Yoke of Christ and Other Sermons* (New York: Harper & Row, Publishers, 1958), pp. 182-192.